Tapestries of Life

The Journey of a Lifetime

Charles E. Cravey

In His Steps Publishing

ISBN: 978-1-58535-035-3 (Paper)

ISBN: 978-1-58535-036-0 (Kindle)

Library of Congress Catalog Number: 2025904036

Cover designed by Charles E. Cravey with Book Brush

Contents

About the author

The Rev. Dr. Charles E. Cravey is a retired ordained minister in the United Methodist Church and has served for fifty-three years in various locations across South Georgia. He has won numerous awards for his writing and mission work. He is a songwriter/singer, having recorded seventeen of his own albums in gospel and country music and writing, producing, and recording many other groups over the years. This is his 30th published book and is his seventh book this month alone!

He is married to Renee Dennis Cravey, and they have two children, Angela Marie Monahan and Jonathan Cravey. They also have two wonderful grandchildren, Benjamin Monahan, and Meghan Monahan. All, except for Jonathan, live in Statesboro, Georgia. Renee and Charles are active members of the First United Methodist Church in Statesboro.

At seventy-three, Dr. Cravey continues to write at a steady pace and has projected many more books soon.

Amazon.com carries all of Dr. Cravey's books.

https://drcharlescravey.com (You may contact Dr. Cravey personally through the online message board)

Introduction

In the intricate weave of human existence, each thread tells a story. Some tales are vibrant and joyous, while others are subdued and somber. Together, they form the rich tapestry of our lives—a mosaic of moments, memories, and emotions.

Welcome to "Tapestries of Life," a collection of short stories that delve into the myriad experiences that define us. Within these pages, you'll encounter characters who navigate the complexities of love and loss, triumph and defeat, hope and despair. Each story is a unique strand in the greater fabric of life, contributing to the endless pattern of our shared humanity.

As you journey through this anthology, may you find reflections of your own life, reminders of the beauty in the mundane, and inspiration in the strength of the human spirit. Let these stories serve as a reminder that, no matter how different our individual paths may be, we are all part of the same intricate tapestry.

Editor: In His Steps Publishing

1

Tapestries of Life

JONATHAN'S JOURNEY

Jonathan, a young twenty-four-year-old man, has faced significant challenges and trauma in his life. It all started when he was just eighteen, deeply in love with a beautiful young girl who tragically lost her life in an automobile accident along with her family. At nineteen, Jonathan underwent severe stomach surgery that brought him to the brink of death. Losing his father at twenty-one left him with the responsibility of caring for his mother and younger sister. Despite these hardships, the college rejected Jonathan because of his inadequate grades, disappointing his determination to pursue higher education. Through it all, Jonathan has shown resilience and strength in the face of adversity, shaping him into the person he is today.

Jonathan faced a challenging time in his life when his friends deserted him just when he needed their support the most. Despite this setback, he did not give up on his dreams. Unable to attend college, he enrolled in a two-year program at the local technical school to learn the carpenter's trade. Throughout the program, Jonathan dedicated himself to mastering various skills, including framing, sheet rocking, plumbing, electrical work, heating and ventilation systems, and crew management. His hard work and determination made him a skilled carpenter with diverse abilities beneficial for future endeavors.

In those harsh days, Jonathan faced challenges like Joseph in Genesis 45:3-11. Despite the difficulties, Jonathan never lost hope and held onto the belief that God had a plan for him. His perseverance and faith in God's providence paid off when he successfully graduated from technical school. Shortly after, a local construction crew recognized his hard work and hired him without hesitation.

Jonathan's positive attitude and strong work ethic quickly endeared him to his co-workers, who saw in him a kindred spirit. The construction projects under his supervision thrived, thanks to his leadership and dedication. Impressed by his capabilities, the company promoted Jonathan to the position of foreman, where he managed two separate crews of workers in the town. Jonathan's journey from struggling individual to a respected leader serves as a testament to the power of determination and faith in overcoming life's challenges.

As fate would have it, Jonathan eventually found himself in a position to help those very people who had wronged him years before. George, who had failed in college, sought work with Jonathan's company without realizing that Jonathan was the man in charge. Despite their past, Jonathan's kind heart led him to hire George immediately, offering him a second chance. Leroy, who had married and soon after divorced, fell on tough times, struggling to maintain stable employment. However, Jonathan extended a helping hand and took Leroy in, despite the betrayal Leroy had inflicted on him in the past. That Jonathan would even consider helping those who had deserted him overwhelmed Leroy, highlighting the power of redemption and forgiveness in their story.

Jonathan had learned to find solace in the words of Psalm 37:1–11. Through righteous living, God sustained Jonathan and taught him to be patient and kind, even if life seemed unfair. God, he felt, would provide, and protect him, just like the psalmist promised. His crew all loved Jonathan and worked even harder under his leadership. The reunion renewed old acquaintances and friendships.

As Jonathan continued to meditate on the verses of Psalm 37, he found strength in the teachings of the scripture. The words guided him in deciding and facing challenges with a calm heart. Jonathan's faith in God's provision and protection grew stronger each day, influencing his actions and interactions with those around him.

Under Jonathan's leadership, his crew thrived, inspired by his dedication and compassion. They worked diligently, united by a common purpose and a shared respect for their captain. Old acquaintances and friendships brought Jonathan's crew joy and nostalgia, renewing bonds forged through shared experiences and hardships.

Through the power of Psalm 37, faith, perseverance, and the enduring belief that righteousness would prevail in the end marked Jonathan's journey.

Jonathan's faith in the resurrection (I Corinthians 15:35-38, 42-50) gave him hope and strength. He faced each day with purpose. His profound spiritual convictions provided him with an inner peace that he had not experienced before. Despite enduring various traumas in his life, Jonathan's faith had grown stronger, equipping him to confront any challenges that the world presented.

Jonathan's faith in the resurrection and eternal life, as outlined in I Corinthians 15:35-38, 42-50, served as a beacon of hope for him. This belief instilled in him a sense of purpose and direction, enabling him to navigate through life's difficulties with resilience. He found solace in the promise of eternal life, knowing that his trials and tribulations were temporary in the grand scheme of things.

Through his unwavering faith, Jonathan discovered a newfound strength that empowered him to face adversity head-on. The challenges he had overcome only deepened his faith and solidified his trust in a higher power. This inner strength allowed him to approach each day with courage and determination, no longer shackled by fear or doubt.

Jonathan's journey is a testament to the transformative power of faith and belief in the face of life's uncertainties. His unwavering trust in the resurrection and eternal life provided him with a renewed sense of purpose and inner peace. Through his experiences, Jonathan learned that adversity can be a catalyst for spiritual growth and that faith can be a guiding light in times of darkness.

In his journey of faith, Jonathan delved deep into the teachings found in Luke 6:27–38, which profoundly impacted his life. Through these verses, he learned the powerful lesson of loving his enemies, extending forgiveness to those who wronged him, and embracing a spirit of generosity. Despite the challenges he faced, Jonathan discovered immense rewards in applying Jesus' teachings to his life. The joy and fulfillment he experienced from living a life grounded in love and mercy were truly transformative.

Jonathan's journey exemplifies the transformative power of faith and the teachings of Jesus. By internalizing the principles of love, forgiveness, and generosity, he could navigate life's obstacles with grace and compassion. Through his actions, Jonathan not only found peace and fulfillment but also became a source of inspiration and positivity for those around him. His story serves as a testament to the enduring impact of faith and the profound changes it can bring to an individual's life.

As Jonathan continued to walk in faith, his life became a living testimony to God's providence and the significance of righteous living. Through his unwavering commitment to following Christ, he found assurance in the promise of rewards for the faithful and the hope of resurrection and eternal life. Jonathan's story beautifully illustrates these timeless truths, intricately woven together by the guiding hand of a loving and merciful God.

Jonathan's life was now a tapestry, made from the faith of a loving God who rescued and set him on a fresh path.

2

"Ice Cream is Cheaper than Therapy!"

———⧓———

I was visiting my local Dairy Queen the other day when I noticed a simple yet thought-provoking sign on the outside marquee that read, "Ice Cream is Cheaper than Therapy." I immediately thought of how weird the sign was and laughed at it as I walked inside. But then I thought of how such a lighthearted saying held an even deeper thought about how our society approaches today's mental health and self-care.

This simple phrase juxtaposes two concepts that seem unrelated. While ice cream is a beloved treat that conjures up thoughts of happiness and indulgence, it contrasts with thoughts of therapy for those suffering with a mental health concern. That comparison invites us to consider the emotional relief that both can offer.

My wife is a big "Blizzard" fan! She loves all varieties that Dairy Queen offers. My favorite is the peanut butter parfait. For as long as I can remember, there has been that sweet treat in my life. I recall the very day that the Dairy Queen opened in my hometown. That was a glorious celebration for me, for I had long desired to get the peanut butter parfait I had heard about!

For Americans, at least, ice cream has been a symbol of inner comfort and happiness. In the dead heat of South Georgia summers, an ice cream cone, or Blizzard, evokes senses of nostalgia and contentment. Ice cream brings people together and creates shared moments of joy. Therefore, the Dairy Queen sign suggests that sometimes the simple pleasures in life can provide us with a temporary escape from the stresses of life. Americans have more stress than other countries in the world. Our mental health clinics are overflowing with people who need mental health.

We rank low on the list of the world's happiest countries. What is wrong with us? Why are we stressed all the time?

I remember a few years ago when work and personal responsibilities overwhelmed me. It only took one trip to the local Dairy Queen and my problems just seemed to float away, at least for fifteen minutes! It was an effortless way I had to take care of myself.

While the DQ sign suggests that ice cream is a cheaper alternative to therapy, we must recognize the profound value of professional mental health support. That support gives us a safe space to explore our thoughts and feelings, develop coping strategies, and even work through the personal challenges we face daily. As Proverbs 11:14 reminds us, "Where no counsel is, the people fall; but in the multitude of counselors there is safety."

To me, the DQ sign doesn't undermine the need for mental healthcare but stresses the universal need for relief and comfort in our lives. If we go around all bottled up within ourselves, we will eventually develop cracks in our lives. Who will mend those cracks? I suggest qualified counselors and God, who is the chief counselor!

In America, at least, there is the problem of cost to someone seeking mental healthcare. It can be prohibitively expensive and difficult to access. It is an unfortunate reality that, for some, having that tasty treat of ice cream is more affordable and accessible than most mental health services. In Matthew 11:28, Jesus offers an invitation to those who are struggling: "Come unto me, all ye that labor and are heavy laden, and I will give you rest." It may sound fanciful, but I've found that just being in the presence of a church worship service gives me pause and an uplifted spirit.

The D.Q. sign also serves to remind us we should practice self-care in various forms. Professional therapy is invaluable, but it is also crucial to care for those small, everyday actions that contribute to our overall well-being. Having a treat to enjoy, walking in the park, spending time with your loved ones—these pleasures can bring us respite and much-needed joy. As I Corinthians 6:19-20 reminds us, our bodies are temples of the Holy Spirit, and thus, we are called to honor God by taking care of ourselves.

My friend (Joe) was really going through a tough uphill battle in his life when he approached me one day as his pastor. I dropped everything I was doing and drove him to our local Dairy Queen and bought him the ice cream of his choice. We enjoyed the ice cream and our time of sharing with each other, and soon I could see the tension slowly lifting from his shoulders. Our time together, of course, did not solve his tremendous problems that day but gave Joe some much-needed relief amid a terrible day. Later, Joe sought therapy, but that day at Dairy Queen was a small but meaningful step in his journey to healing.

In a world filled with stress and anxiety, the phrase "Ice Cream is Cheaper than Therapy" serves as a reminder to find joy in the simple pleasures of life. While the whimsical message resonates with many, it also highlights the importance of addressing our mental health needs. Both indulging in a scoop of ice cream and seeking therapy play crucial roles in our journey towards emotional wellbeing.

Ice cream symbolizes comfort and delight, offering a temporary escape from the pressures of daily life. Its sweetness can uplift our spirits and provide moments of happiness amidst chaos. On the other hand, therapy serves as a structured approach to understanding and managing our emotions. It provides a safe space to explore our thoughts, feelings, and experiences, leading to personal growth and healing.

Proverbs 17:22 beautifully captures the essence of this duality: "A merry heart doeth good like a medicine, but a broken spirit drieth the bones." It reminds us that both joy and healing are essential components of a healthy mind and soul. By embracing the small joys of life while acknowledging the need for professional support, we can cultivate a balanced approach to emotional well-being.

In conclusion, let us cherish the moments of happiness that ice cream brings while also recognizing the value of therapy in nurturing our mental health. Finding a harmonious blend of indulgence and introspection can lead us towards a more fulfilling and resilient life.

So, instead of depressing over the issues you have or are facing in life, take some time for yourself. Seek a friend or pastor to share your feelings with. If possible, seek help from a qualified mental health counselor. It will do you good. And don't forget, DQ can give you a sweet and cool respite from the trials of life! Tell them I sent you.

3

The Magic of Manure

M y father taught me a lot about the art of farming. While plowing with Betsy, our old mule, my father would select a distant landmark, like a fence post or tree, for me to aim for. In that fashion, I would lay a straight row. Often, I would fail because something else would catch my attention and cause me to look away. His lessons were to keep my eye on the goal ahead of me, never looking back or away from distractions in life. There is a wealth of knowledge to be learned from farming.

The first time I plowed Betsy, my dad looked at the poor row I made because a rabbit running across the field had distracted me. That evening, I suffered the stripes of a peach tree switch on my legs, undergirding my father's lesson about keeping my eyes on the goal. I have since applied that lesson almost daily as I've maneuvered through life.

In the deep south, farmers have a unique approach to preparing their fields for seed planting: manure. Despite the pungent odor it creates, many farmers value manure as a resource. One farmer famously remarked, "It smells like money!" The benefits of using manure as fertilizer are immense. Not only does it enhance the quality of the soil and promote crop growth, but it is also a cost-effective alternative to traditional fertilizers. Many farmers are turning back to this age-old practice because of its affordability and proven results. People believe that even a handful of this magical fertilizer can transform even the most infertile lands into thriving fields. It's usually made from cow and chicken waste, and it smells terrible!

Old Man Johnson stood at the edge of his field one day and watched the tractor distributors spread manure across his fields, knowing it was necessary to produce a crop.

Johnson was a seasoned old farmer with calloused hands and a rusty smile. He had spent years tilling the earth, but his spirit was unyielding.

Guided by his faith and the verse "Let us not become weary in well doing," Farmer Johnson worked his land in the quiet countryside. He knew that at the proper time, he would reap a harvest. Would the rain arrive on time? Could he settle his bills for fertilizers, seeds, and irrigation equipment? Despite his fretting, Farmer Johnson surrendered his crops to divine providence.

In today's agricultural landscape, farming grows increasingly difficult. Corporate farms loom large, monopolizing vast swathes of land and streamlining operations with modern machinery. The exorbitant prices of tractors often put them out of reach for many, leaving only the most affluent to prosper. However, Farmer Johnson remained steadfast in his commitment to traditional methods, using the rich manure from his chicken coops as a natural fertilizer for his crops.

Farmer Johnson's prayers mingle with the scent of freshly turned soil as the sun sets over his fields, a testament to his enduring spirit and devotion. He felt an extraordinary pride in his two hundred acres and treated it with love and care.

Farmer Johnson, a seasoned farmer with a wealth of experience passed down from his father, vividly remembers the lessons learned during his upbringing. His father's wise words about the similarities between life and manure still resonate with him to this day. Through the trials of failed crops and the joy of welcoming his children into the world, Farmer Johnson has experienced the full spectrum of life's challenges and rewards. He cherishes memories of kneeling in the fields with his father, seeking divine intervention and guidance during times of need. As he carries on the family farming tradition, Farmer Johnson now relies on his own instincts and knowledge, built upon the foundation laid by his father.

In the quaint town, a bustling seed store served as a hub for local farmers to convene and exchange stories and knowledge. The seasoned farmers would often gather around, engaging in lively discussions and sharing their experiences. Younger farmers highly esteemed Farmer Johnson for his wealth of wisdom and practical advice. One day, he told a memorable tale of a brutal winter where they saved their crops by strategically using manure. The younger farmers listened attentively, eager to learn from the trials and triumphs of their predecessors. In this tight-knit community, the seed store became more than just a place to purchase seeds; it was a space where generations came together to chew the fat and pass down valuable lessons from one farmer to another.

In the crowd was a young farmer named Elise. She had taken over her family's farm after her father's death and was struggling mightily to survive. Farmer Johnson pulled her aside and shared James 1:2-4, focusing on the joy found in facing trials. The scripture spoke of perseverance born from testing faith.

It was as if Elise had found a new hope and realized that just as the manure enriched the soil, the many challenges she faced would strengthen her resolve. After Farmer Johnson's illustration, she felt ready to face whatever lay ahead. As the time neared for harvest, Johnson looked out at his fields teeming with life. He realized that the manure had once again worked its magic. The fields were lush and green, and the vines produced a bounty harvest.

Elise's journey mirrored the growth and resilience seen in Farmer Johnson's fields. Just as the challenges she faced enriched her character, the manure enriched the soil, paving the way for a thriving harvest. This story serves as a reminder that adversity can lead to growth and that, with determination and perseverance, one can overcome any obstacle. The main thing is to keep the main thing the main thing! Keep your eyes on the goal in life and move forward, trusting in the goodness and mercy of the almighty.

The next time you are sitting at a fancy restaurant with family or friends and enjoying a bountiful meal, remember the story of old Farmer Johnson. With your mouth full, never complain about farmers or the lives they live to serve you.

Someone is spreading manure this week near our home because I can smell it miles away! "It smells like money!"

4

The Reflections of a Life

Wilson sat by his bedroom window, mesmerized by the golden hues of the sunrise, painting his garden in warm light. At seventy-nine years old, he had seen countless sunrises, but this one felt different. The flowers in his garden seemed to glow with life, a stark contrast to his own fragile state. Cancer had invaded his body, turning every moment into a precious gift. Wilson had always faced life with determination and zeal, but now, weakened by the disease, he felt the weight of his mortality. As he watched the sunrise, he understood his time on earth was short, each day emphasizing that his end could come at any moment.

Wilson's thoughts began wandering back through the years as he slowly sipped his tea. The words from David's Psalm came to mind: "Yea, though I walk through the valley of the shadow of death, I will fear no evil, for thou art with me, thy rod and thy staff, they comfort me." He had leaned upon the promises of Psalm 23 for years and now hoped it would guide him through these dark days of his life and offer any solace possible in his moments of despair.

Wilson's life had been a tapestry of both joy and sorrow. When he met Doris at a church gathering, it was the happiest day of his life. She was infectious with her kindness and laughter and could make anyone contagious. Their little three-bedroom house had been a haven of blessings, and they both had built it with love, faith, and countless adventures. The house was on the edge of town, nestled in a quiet neighborhood surrounded by trees and flowers. There, they had raised three beautiful children, each with their own unique personalities and talents. Wilson and Doris had created a warm and loving home filled with laughter, love, and cherished memories. The walls echoed with the sound of children playing, the aroma of home-cooked meals, and the comfort of family gatherings. Despite the challenges they faced along the way, Wilson and Doris remained steadfast in their commitment to each other and their family, finding strength in their shared experiences and unwavering love.

He recalled a particular spring day while he and Doris were sitting on the porch swing. The sun was gleaming, casting a warm glow over the blooming flowers in their garden. As they swayed back and forth on the swing, Doris suddenly quoted a verse from Jeremiah 29:11: "For I know the thoughts that I think toward you, saith the Lord, thoughts of peace, and not of evil, to give you an expected end." Those words had become their mantra, a source of comfort and inspiration during challenging times. They offered hope, solace, and the reminder that they were never alone in their journey through life's difficulties.

Wilson was deeply affected by the passing of his beloved wife, Doris, who had lost her battle with cancer a decade ago. Her death created a profound void in Wilson's heart, leaving him with a sense of loss and longing. Despite the pain, Wilson found solace in his faith in God, often drawing strength from the words of John 14:2–3: "In my Father's house are many mansions; if it were not so, would I have told you I go to prepare a place for you? And if I go and prepare a place for you, I will come again and will take you to myself, that where I am there you may be also." These verses provided Wilson with a sense of hope and comfort, as he held onto the belief that one day he would be reunited with Doris in a place of eternal peace and happiness. Their shared memories and the love that had bound them together for so long fueled Wilson's desire to see Doris again, keeping their connection alive in his heart and mind.

As with most of us, Wilson was contemplating what legacy he would leave behind. The stories he had shared with his children, of course, would be lessons in life he hoped they would carry forward.

He and his granddaughter, Michelle, were talking one day, and she asked Wilson about the secret to a happy life. He simply shared with her a quote from Proverbs 3:5-6, which says, "Trust in the Lord with all thine heart; and lean not unto thine own understanding; in all thy ways acknowledge him, and he shall direct thy paths." Michelle had marveled at her granddad's ability to quote scriptures without having his Bible.

During his illness, Wilson found solace and strength in his unwavering faith. Referencing 2 Corinthians 4:16-18, he held onto the words that spoke to his heart: "For which cause we faint not; but though our outward man perish, yet the inward man is renewed day by day. For our light affliction, which is but for a moment, worketh for us a far more exceeding and eternal weight of glory. While we look not at the things which are seen, but at the things which are not seen; for the things which are seen are temporal; but the things which are not seen are eternal." These verses became Wilson's guiding light, reminding him to focus on the eternal rather than the temporary and to find renewal in the face of his physical decline. Wilson's faith served as his stronghold and anchor, providing him with unwavering hope and comfort during his challenging journey.

As the sun had fully risen, casting a warm glow over Wilson's weathered face, he found solace in the gentle embrace of its rays. With a heart filled with gratitude, he closed his tired eyes and whispered a prayer of thanksgiving for the life he had lived. Memories of love shared with Doris flooded his mind, warming his soul even in the fading light of his years. Through the trials and triumphs, it was his unwavering faith that had sustained him, a beacon of hope in the darkest of times.

Drifting off into a peaceful sleep, Wilson felt a profound sense of tranquility washing over him. The whispers of the wind carried messages of reassurance, as if nature itself were soothing his weary spirit. In that moment, he knew that his earthly journey, though nearing its end, had been but a prelude to something greater. The promise of an eternal reunion with Doris and his Creator filled him with a sense of peace that transcended all understanding.

As the day turned into night, Wilson's breathing slowed, his chest rising and falling in a steady rhythm. Serene stillness filled the room, broken only by the soft rustle of leaves outside the window. In that quiet moment, Wilson surrendered to the embrace of sleep, ready to embark on the last leg of his journey, guided by the light of love and faith that had illuminated his path thus far.

5

Overcoming Adversity

I have been faithfully watching a singing group on YouTube called "Brothers of the Heart." They are simply fantastic and caught my attention immediately because of two people in the group, Bradley Walker, and Gordon Mote. The four singers in the group are Jimmy Fortune of the Statler Brothers, Bradley Walker, Mike Rogers, and Ben Isaacs of the Gospel family, The Isaacs. The group's harmony and musicianship are excellent and are a joy to listen to. I applaud their tremendous success.

Brothers of the Heart is a captivating singing group that has garnered a loyal following on YouTube. Their harmonious blend of voices and exceptional musicianship make their performances a genuine delight for music enthusiasts. It is truly inspiring to witness the success and artistry of *Brothers of the Heart*.

Gordon Mote, the talented pianist for the group, has a remarkable story of overcoming challenges. Born blind, Gordon defied the odds to pursue his passion for music. With dedication and hard work, he honed his skills to become a fantastic pianist. Having played numerous sessions in Nashville studios, Gordon has also recorded several successful album projects. His talent and perseverance have earned him admiration from singers and musicians around the world, as well as within the Nashville music scene.

Bradley Walker, the bass singer of the group, sits in his wheelchair on stage and delivers a deep and wonderful voice. Bradley was born with a form of muscular dystrophy. Through therapy and hard work, Bradley continues his passion for music and has never looked back. Bradley has proven that physical limitations cannot stifle one's artistic spirit.

Despite the challenges he faced from early on, Bradley Walker refused to let his circumstances define him. His determination and love for music drove him to push through the pain and limitations. With each note he sings, Bradley not only captivates his audience with his powerful voice but also inspires them with his resilience and perseverance.

Over the years, Bradley has become a symbol of hope for many individuals facing similar obstacles. Through his music, he spreads a message of strength and courage, showing that with dedication and passion, anything is possible. Bradley's story serves as a reminder that true artistry knows no boundaries and that one's creativity can transcend any physical limitations.

In a world where adversity can often seem insurmountable, Bradley Walker stands as a beacon of light, highlighting the transformative power of music and the human spirit. His journey serves as a testament to the fact that, with steadfast determination and a deep love for one's craft, individuals can overcome even the most daunting challenges. Bradley's story is a reminder to us all that, within every setback, lies an opportunity for greatness and that true artistry knows no bounds.

Challenges and obstacles are always inevitable in our world. The stories of those who triumph over adversity always move us. These stories, like those of Walker and Motes, never fail to inspire us.

Brothers of the Heart are a splendid example of how passion, resilience, and determination can overcome even the most daunting disabilities. Their journey serves as a beacon of hope for many facing similar struggles.

Stories abound of musicians, singers, and athletes who have overcome tremendous odds to achieve remarkable success. From winning Olympic medals to recording chart-topping songs, authoring inspirational books, and accomplishing other impressive feats, these individuals display the power of determination and perseverance. Witnessing their abilities and achievements against all odds fills us with awe and motivates us to face our own challenges with courage and resilience.

Brothers of the Heart are a remarkable supergroup that combines elements of country, gospel, and bluegrass music to create a unique and powerful sound. Composed of talented musicians who have each overcome personal challenges, the group's music is a testament to the strength of collaboration and support. Through their beautiful harmonies and fresh interpretations of classic songs, *Brothers of the Heart* offer a message of hope and resilience to their listeners.

Tracks like "Listen to the Music" and "Gentle on My Mind" exemplify the group's exceptional talent and unwavering dedication to their craft. With their music, the group not only entertains but also inspires those who may face their own struggles.

Philippians 4:13 serves as a powerful reminder of the strength that comes from faith. This verse, "I can do all things through Christ who strengthens me," emphasizes the belief that with God's support and guidance, we can overcome any challenge or obstacle that comes our way. It instills a sense of empowerment and resilience, inspiring individuals to persevere in the face of adversity. This message comforts and motivates many, reminding them of the unyielding support and strength their faith provides.

In Isaiah 40:31, it is stated, "But they that wait upon the Lord shall renew their strength; they shall mount up with wings as eagles; they shall run, and not be weary; and they shall walk, and not faint." This verse speaks to the promise of strength and endurance for those who place their trust and hope in the Lord. It illustrates a powerful image of being able to soar high like eagles, run without becoming tired, and walk without experiencing fatigue. This passage serves as a reminder of the steady support and sustenance that come from having faith in God. It encourages individuals to rely on the Lord for strength in times of weakness and to find comfort in the assurance that He will provide the fortitude to overcome any challenges that may come their way.

2 Corinthians 12:9-10 states: "My grace is sufficient for thee: for my strength is made perfect in weakness. Most gladly therefore will I rather glory in my infirmities, that the power of Christ may rest upon me."

This powerful verse from the Bible reminds us that in our moments of weakness, we can find strength through the grace of God. It teaches us to embrace our vulnerabilities and shortcomings, for it is in these moments that the power of Christ can truly shine through. By acknowledging our weaknesses and relying on the grace of God, we allow His strength to work through us and guide us on our journey of faith.

These scriptures all relate to people like Gordon Motes and Bradley Walker, reinforcing the message that faith and determination can help overcome any obstacles in life.

Gordon Motes and Bradley Walker exemplify persistent dedication to their craft, despite their disabilities. Their journeys serve as a powerful reminder that challenges do not define us; rather, it is our passion, perseverance, and resilience that shape our true potential.

Gordon Motes and Bradley Walker show that, with faith and determination, one can overcome any obstacle. Their achievements serve as a source of inspiration for others, reminding us to not let challenges hinder our progress. Instead, we should embrace our obstacles, using them as opportunities to grow stronger and more resilient. Let us celebrate their accomplishments and draw motivation from their journeys to face our own challenges with the same determination and grace.

As we reflect on the journeys of Gordon Motes and Bradley Walker, let their examples of faith, determination, and resilience encourage us to face our obstacles. Just as they have shown us, challenges do not have to define us; rather, they can serve as steppingstones to our true potential. May their stories inspire us to keep pushing forward, knowing that with God's strength and our constant dedication, we can overcome any obstacles that come our way.

You've heard the old saying, "I used to complain about having holes in my shoes, until I saw a man with no feet."

It is easy to get caught up in our own struggles and setbacks, often losing sight of the blessings that surround us. However, when we take a moment to look beyond our own circumstances, we realize the abundance of things we must be thankful for. From the simple joys of everyday life to the opportunities and resources at our disposal, there is much to appreciate.

The saying emphasizes the resilience and strength of the human spirit. Despite facing obstacles and limitations, we can rise above our adversities and achieve remarkable feats. It serves as a reminder that our strengths do not define us, but they shape us into stronger, more resilient individuals.

In conclusion, let us remember to count our blessings, no matter how small they may seem. By cultivating a mindset of gratitude and perspective, we can navigate life's challenges with grace and resilience. Like the man with no feet who inspired the saying, may we too find the strength to overcome our obstacles and achieve greatness in our own unique ways.

6

A Chickadee's Dilemma

❖

A sudden, loud thump on our patio windows disrupted the peaceful atmosphere the other day as I sat nestled in my favorite recliner, engrossed in an enjoyable book. Startled, our dog Sassy began barking furiously, drawing my attention to the commotion outside. While I peered through the window, I saw a small chickadee lying motionless on the porch after hitting the glass pane during a heavy rainstorm.

Feeling a wave of sympathy for the injured bird, I hurried outside to assess the situation. With gentle hands, I carefully lifted the little chickadee, sadly noticing its broken leg bent at an unnatural angle. Initially fearing the worst for the fragile creature, I sought solace in the company of my partner Renee, who was amid painting a serene landscape in our workshop. Showing her the injured bird, we both shared a moment of concern for its well-being, offering a heartfelt prayer for its recovery.

We unexpectedly encountered nature's vulnerability. This fleeting moment filled us with compassion and a sense of connection to life's delicate balance, highlighting the beauty and fragility of all living things.

As I was walking back to the porch, the little fellow rose and began clinging to the side of my hand with one leg. Its delicate feathers and bright eyes made my heart melt. Within moments, the bird mustered up its strength and flew off into our yard's underbrush, disappearing into the lush greenery. I couldn't help but feel a sense of joy and gratitude for being able to assist the little bird in its moment of need. This simple yet meaningful encounter with nature reminded me of the beauty and interconnectedness of all living beings.

We are all interconnected in this world. Our actions, thoughts, and choices have ripple effects that extend beyond ourselves, shaping the world around us. From the relationships we cultivate to the impact we have on the environment, every decision we make contributes to the intricate web of connections that bind us together. This interconnectedness reminds us of our shared humanity and the importance of considering the well-being of others in all that we do. By recognizing and embracing our interconnectedness, we can work towards creating a more harmonious and sustainable world for all.

To accomplish a more harmonious world, we must prioritize understanding, empathy, and cooperation among individuals and nations. We can achieve this by fostering open communication, promoting diversity and inclusivity, and resolving conflicts peacefully. Education plays a crucial role in promoting tolerance and acceptance of diverse cultures and perspectives.

Promoting sustainable practices and environmental stewardship can help create a more equitable and peaceful world for future generations. It is through collective effort and a shared commitment to peace and understanding that we can work towards a more harmonious world.

To create a more sustainable world for all, collaboration and collective effort are essential. We can achieve this through a combination of individual actions, community involvement, and global initiatives. Individuals can contribute by adopting sustainable practices in their daily lives, such as reducing waste, conserving energy, and supporting environmentally friendly products. Communities can work together to implement sustainable projects such as community gardens, recycling programs, and clean-up initiatives. At a global level, governments, organizations, and businesses can collaborate on policies and practices that promote sustainability, such as investing in renewable energy, reducing carbon emissions, and protecting natural resources. By working together at all levels, we can create a more sustainable world that benefits both current and future generations.

One of our cherished annual traditions is putting out the bluebird boxes that Renee and I have lovingly built for our beautiful bluebirds. These boxes get placed strategically approximately one hundred yards apart, as recommended by the Audubon Society. This spacing helps ensure that the bluebirds have ample nesting opportunities while minimizing competition and territorial disputes.

We take immense pleasure in observing the bluebirds as they visit each box, meticulously exploring their options before selecting the perfect spot to build their nest. Their presence brings us immense joy, and we find great fulfillment in providing a safe and welcoming habitat for these delightful creatures.

Several years ago, I had four honeybee boxes in our yard, providing us with delicious honey for many seasons. However, our peaceful coexistence with the bees ended abruptly when Renee got stung under one eye while tending to our flowers. She insisted it was me or the bees, and despite my reluctance, they had to go.

Determined to ensure the well-being of the bees, I found a wonderful children's park located approximately fifty miles away. I donated the bees and the boxes to the park, where they could educate schoolchildren about the importance of these pollinators. Although it was a sad farewell, I took solace in knowing that the bees would continue to thrive in their new home, spreading knowledge and awareness for generations to come.

The fish in our neighbor's pond appeared to be neglected. We therefore asked the owner if we could take on the responsibility of feeding them. After receiving the owner's approval, Renee and I began feeding the fish daily. Over time, the fish became accustomed to our presence and started coming up to the surface to greet us. This simple act of kindness towards the fish has brought us joy and a sense of fulfillment. We believe that every small deed, such as caring for these fish, contributes to the protection of our planet and its precious creatures.

Ways to make a positive impact on the world from your own backyard:

1. Plant native trees and flowers to provide habitat for local wildlife and support biodiversity.

2. Start a compost pile to reduce waste and create nutrients for the soil in your garden.

3. Install a rain barrel to collect rainwater for watering plants, reducing the demand on municipal water supplies.

4. Set up a bird feeder and bird bath to attract and support local bird populations.

5. Create a small vegetable garden to grow your own food, reducing reliance on imported produce and lowering your carbon footprint.

6. Use eco-friendly lawn care practices, such as using natural fertilizers and avoiding chemical pesticides.

7. Reduce energy consumption by installing solar-powered outdoor lights or a clothesline for drying laundry.

8. Encourage sustainable practices in your community by sharing your knowledge and experiences with neighbors and friends.

In doing some of these things, you will learn the importance of being good stewards in God's amazing world. Why not begin today?

You may not think that the saving of one little chickadee makes a difference, but it did to the chickadee!

God bless you on your journey today.

7

Muscles

Body muscles are vital body parts that play a crucial role in the overall function and movement of the human body. They generate the force needed for physical activities such as walking, running, and lifting objects. Muscles help maintain posture, support the skeletal system, and protect internal organs. Without muscles, the body could not perform the basic functions necessary for survival. Overall, muscles are integral to our daily activities and overall well-being.

Bodybuilders are often a source of envy for many, as their dedication to building muscles is truly admirable.

Whether seen on TV or encountered on the street, their impressive physique serves as a testament to the time and effort they invest in their training. The sight of a bodybuilder can spark feelings of admiration and motivation in onlookers, inspiring them to consider their own fitness goals and the level of commitment required to achieve comparable results. The discipline and hard work shown by bodybuilders serve as a reminder of the rewards that come with perseverance and a focused approach to physical fitness.

Bodybuilding is a physically demanding sport that requires dedication, discipline, and perseverance. The journey to develop a physique like that of a professional bodybuilder such as Hulk Hogan is difficult. It involves intense training sessions, strict dieting, and a significant amount of sacrifice. Bodybuilders push their bodies to the limit, often enduring intense pain and discomfort to achieve their desired results. Besides the physical challenges, bodybuilders also face mental hurdles along the way. The pressure to improve and maintain a certain physique can take a toll on their mental well-being. Body image issues, self-doubt, and the fear of not meeting expectations are common struggles for many bodybuilders. Despite the pain and challenges they face, bodybuilders are driven by their passion for the sport and their desire to achieve their goals. Their dedication and determination set them apart and allow them to transform their bodies into works of art.

The Bible provides specific guidance on how to nurture and develop the body and mind. The Bible's teachings emphasize the importance of holistic well-being, highlighting the interconnectedness of these aspects of human existence. By following the principles and values outlined in the Bible, individuals can work towards achieving balance and harmony in their physical, spiritual, and mental lives. The scriptures offer wisdom and insight on how to care for one's body through healthy living practices, nurture the soul through faith and spiritual growth, and cultivate the mind through education and critical thinking. Overall, the Bible serves as a comprehensive guide for building a solid foundation for overall well-being and fulfillment.

One scripture that emphasizes this is specifically from the book of Psalms. In Psalms 23:1-3, it says, "The Lord is my shepherd; I shall not want. He maketh me to lie down in green pastures; he leadeth me beside the still waters. He restoreth my soul." This passage illustrates the concept of God's provision and guidance in our lives, symbolized by the image of a shepherd caring for his sheep. It highlights the idea of trust, contentment, and spiritual nourishment that come from having a relationship with God.

Physical Bodybuilding Scriptures:

1 Corinthians 9:24-27

"Know ye not that they which run in a race run all, but one receiveth the prize? So run, that ye may obtain. And every man that striveth for the mastery is temperate in all things. Now they do it to obtain a corruptible crown; but we an incorruptible. I therefore so run, not as uncertainly; so fight I, not as one that beateth the air: But I keep under my body, and bring it into subjection; lest that by any means, when I have preached to others, I myself should be a castaway."

1 Timothy 4:8

"For bodily exercise profiteth little; but godliness is profitable unto all things, having promise of the life that now is, and of that which is to come."

Spiritual Building:

Ephesians 6:10-11

"Finally, my brethren, be strong in the Lord, and in the power of his might. Put on the whole armour of God, that ye may be able to stand against the wiles of the devil."

1 Corinthians 3:16-17

"Know ye not that ye are the temple of God and that the Spirit of God dwelleth in you? If any man defile the temple of God, him shall God destroy; for the temple of God is holy, which temple ye are."

Philippians 3:13-14

"Brethren, I count not myself to have apprehended: but this one thing I do, forgetting those things which are behind, and reaching forth unto those things which are before."

Connecting the Two:

Discipline is essential for achieving growth and progress in various aspects of life, including spiritual development. Just as physical training requires a strict regimen to build strength and endurance, spiritual growth demands consistent effort and dedication. This involves engaging in regular spiritual practices such as prayer, meditation, and studying the scriptures to deepen one's connection with the divine and nurture the soul.

Prayer is a powerful tool that allows individuals to communicate with a higher power, express gratitude, seek guidance, and find inner peace. By incorporating prayer into daily routines, individuals can cultivate a sense of spiritual discipline and connection to the divine.

Meditation is a practice that involves quieting the mind, focusing on the present moment, and cultivating mindfulness. Through regular meditation sessions, individuals can enhance their spiritual awareness, reduce stress, and develop a deeper understanding of themselves and their place in the universe.

Studying sacred texts and scriptures is another vital aspect of spiritual discipline. By delving into the teachings and wisdom contained in these texts, we can gain insights, inspiration, and guidance for navigating life's challenges and cultivating spiritual growth.

Discipline plays a crucial role in fostering spiritual growth and deepening one's connection with the divine. By incorporating regular spiritual practices such as prayer, meditation, and studying the scriptures into daily routines, individuals can embark on a journey of self-discovery, inner peace, and spiritual enlightenment.

Perseverance is a quality that encompasses the ability to overcome challenges and push through obstacles to achieve greater strength, whether it be physical or spiritual. It is the unwavering commitment to continue moving forward, even in the face of adversity. Perseverance is not about avoiding difficulties but about confronting them head-on with determination and resilience. By persevering through hardships, individuals can develop a deeper sense of inner strength and fortitude. This quality is essential for personal growth and success in all aspects of life. Through perseverance, individuals can unlock their full potential and reach new heights of achievement.

Transformation: Bodybuilders transform their bodies through dedication and hard work, while spiritual seekers transform their hearts and minds through faith and devotion.

Larry was passionate about his physical fitness. He hit the gym religiously as often as possible. Many envied his unwavering dedication as he sculpted his body with extremely intense workouts. He pushed the limits, for he felt that was when the body responded and changed for him. The weight room was his sanctuary of discipline, endurance, and transformation.

Larry began feeling empty within his soul one day that his physical training could not resolve. His friend (another fitness guru) introduced Larry to the concept of spiritual building. With that, Larry began trying the same principles of bodybuilding to his spiritual journey. It was as if a veil lifted from his eyes. He felt renewed and invigorated.

Larry began a daily spiritual practice to complement his body-building regimen. He started each day with prayer and meditation before his exercise routine. He immersed himself in the scriptures and drew strength and inspiration from scriptures like Ephesians 6:10–11, which encouraged him to put on the full armor of God.

He had learned to incorporate the two disciplines and quickly became a whole person. He now exercised both his spirit and his body during those two most important times of his day. His transformation gave him a profound sense of peace and purpose, and he began sharing what he had learned with others, even teaching a class on bodybuilding and spirit-building. He showed how dedication, perseverance, and a willingness to face and overcome obstacles intertwined the two.

God bless you on your journey today.

8

Seeing is Believing

The Gospel of John, specifically John 20:30–31, mentions that Jesus performed many signs before his disciples, not all of which the book records. However, the ones that are written serve a specific purpose—to strengthen the reader's belief in Jesus as the Christ, the Son of God. It is through this belief that one can attain eternal life through his name. This passage highlights the importance of faith and the miraculous deeds of Jesus in solidifying that faith.

The tomb where they buried Jesus after his crucifixion forms the setting of John 20. It is early in the morning on the first day of the week, and Mary Magdalene goes to the tomb and finds the stone rolled away. She then runs to tell Peter and another disciple, who sees the empty tomb for themselves. Mary stays behind and encounters Jesus, who reveals himself to her. This chapter in the Bible narrates the events following Jesus' resurrection, including his appearances to his disciples and the doubt of Thomas.

It is to Thomas that Jesus invokes the passage in John 20:30–31. In these verses, Jesus appears to his disciples after the resurrection, and Thomas, who had doubted the resurrection, is present. Jesus shows Thomas his wounds, and Thomas believes. Jesus then says to Thomas, "Because you have seen me, you have believed; blessed are those who have not seen and yet have believed." This passage highlights the importance of faith and belief in Jesus' teachings, even without physical proof.

In our quest for understanding belief, a fundamental question arises: how many of us honestly believe without the influence of a sign or feeling? This inquiry compels us to reflect on the essence of belief and the impact of firsthand experiences on our convictions. It is a frequent practice in our daily lives to seek reassurance or affirmation of our beliefs through concrete signs or emotional encounters.

Belief is a deeply ingrained aspect of human consciousness that guides our thoughts, actions, and perceptions of the world. It serves as a foundational framework through which we interpret reality and make sense of our existence. However, the origins of our beliefs are multifaceted, influenced by a myriad of factors, including upbringing, culture, education, and individual experiences.

Among these factors, firsthand experiences hold a unique and powerful sway over our beliefs. When we encounter a situation or phenomenon firsthand, we can engage with it on a visceral level, drawing upon our senses and emotions to inform our understanding. The significance of firsthand experiences in shaping beliefs lies in their ability to provide a sense of immediacy and authenticity to our convictions. Unlike secondhand information or abstract concepts, firsthand experiences offer a direct and unfiltered encounter with the object of our belief.

Whether it is witnessing a breathtaking natural phenomenon, experiencing a profound moment of connection with another person, or undergoing a life-altering event, these firsthand experiences leave an indelible mark on our psyche, influencing our beliefs in profound ways.

We cannot understate the role of firsthand experiences in shaping our beliefs. Personal encounters build the foundation for our convictions, grounding our beliefs in tangible experience. By acknowledging the power of firsthand experiences in shaping our beliefs, we gain a deeper appreciation for the intricacies of human belief systems and the profound impact of personal encounters on our understanding of the world.

Many people strongly believe in things unseen, even without physical proof. People often explore this concept in discussions of spirituality, religion, and personal convictions. People who believe but have not seen may rely on experiences, teachings, or feelings to support their faith. We often describe this belief as a deep trust in something beyond the tangible and visible aspects of life. It can be a source of strength, comfort, and guidance for many individuals as they navigate their beliefs and values.

Seeing is believing. Faith, however, is better described in Hebrews 11:1: "Now faith is the substance of things hoped for, the evidence of things not seen." Faith is a fundamental aspect of many belief systems and spiritual practices.

It is the unwavering trust and confidence in something beyond what is physically present or clear. The verse from Hebrews emphasizes that faith is not reliant on tangible proof or visible confirmation. Instead, it is the assurance of things hoped for and the conviction of things unseen. This profound statement encapsulates the essence of faith and highlights its transformative power in guiding individuals through uncertainty and adversity. Just as sight provides evidence of the world, faith offers a spiritual lens through which we can perceive the unseen and hold on to hope in the face of challenges.

Some years ago, an incredibly challenging period occurred in my life when I just simply felt as though I had lost everything. I also felt uncertain about the future and where it would lead me. A dear friend of mine, deeply religious in all facets, told me the story of Jesus' miracles and his teachings. I had heard these stories before and had even preached sermons on them. But my friend's telling of the stories opened my eyes to a completely new perspective.

That following Sunday, I attended worship where the pastor preached on Jesus' love and the transformative power of faith. He said that, although we may not witness the physical miracles Jesus performed, we believe they happened, for they helped us find hope and purpose for our lives.

Through his sermon, a sense of peace and clarity came over me I had not felt in a long time. Like the disciples, I, too, could find strength and guidance through my faith in the miracles of Christ.

As I listened, I felt a sense of peace and clarity that I hadn't experienced in a long time. I realized that, like the disciples who witnessed Jesus' signs, I, too, could find strength and guidance through my faith. This moment marked the beginning of a profound spiritual journey for me, where I learned to trust in Jesus and believe in His promise of eternal life all over again.

9

Regularities

John 7:15 - "And the Jews marvelled, saying, How knoweth this man letters, having never learned?"

Have you ever noticed how frequently people point out irregularities in things, but rarely do they mention when something is "regular"? The focus is often on what is out of the ordinary rather than what is consistent and expected. This tendency to highlight irregularities raises the question of how often people acknowledge and appreciate regularity in various aspects of life. This story explores the concept of regularity and how often people recognize and emphasize it in everyday discourse. It deals with a very "touchy" subject — Jesus and the Pharisees.

In this passage, Jesus' wisdom and knowledge surprised the people, as he had not undergone formal religious training. This verse is part of a larger narrative in the Gospel of John that highlights Jesus' teachings and interactions with the Jewish community. Because he was an unknown person with no apparent authority, the Pharisees and other Jewish leaders in the temple openly challenged the legitimacy of his actions and teachings.

1. **The Innocence of Jesus**: Jesus' purity and direct connection to God, untainted by institutional dogma, disturbed the leaders in our story. His teachings often emphasized love, compassion, and understanding rather than strict adherence to ritualistic laws.

2. **Temple Leadership's Rigidity**: Because only the temple leaders had a lock on the Law of God, their interpretations of that Law were strict and created barriers to spiritual enlightenment. Their emphasis on rules over faith's essence, controlled access to divine truth.

3. **Jesus' Revolutionary Approach**: Jesus reinterpreted and fulfilled the laws, providing a deeper spiritual understanding. His actions, such as healing on the Sabbath and befriending societal outcasts, demonstrated the spirit of the law—love and mercy—over its letter.

4. **Shutting Up the Kingdom of Heaven**: The temple leaders' rigidity and insistence on ritual purity often excluded those who needed spiritual guidance the most. Jesus opened the kingdom to everyone, emphasizing faith and repentance over ritual compliance.

5. **Modern Implications**: How do we see this tension between institutional religion and personal faith today? Are there ways in which modern religious institutions might also "shut up the kingdom of heaven"? How can believers today emulate Jesus' approach to faith and inclusivity?

In the historical narrative, Jesus emerged as a disruptive figure, challenging the norms and beliefs of the devotees of *regularity.* His unconventional background, associations, and causes - advocating for the marginalized and vulnerable - clashed with the established order. His actions caused confusion and discomfort among those accustomed to strict adherence to tradition. The temple leaders, through their reactions to Jesus, revealed their true nature, characterized by narrowness, bigotry, and an unwillingness to embrace change. Jesus' presence and actions served as a catalyst for introspection and revealed the underlying prejudices and limitations of the established religious hierarchy.

In the pursuit of preserving the faith, the leaders dedicated years of their lives to this noble cause. They were the guiding lights who took on the responsibility of discerning and overseeing the spiritual journey of their community. Through their unwavering commitment and dedication, they upheld and passed down the values and beliefs of their faith through generations.

The leaders, through their relentless efforts, established themselves as the guardians of the faith. They meticulously documented the teachings and traditions, ensuring their preservation for future generations. Their role extended beyond mere observation; they actively participated in the spiritual growth of their community, guiding individuals on their path towards enlightenment. Their knowledge and wisdom were the key to understanding the complexities of the faith and its practices, and people revered them for it.

The leaders played a crucial role in maintaining the integrity of the faith community. They were the arbiters of morality and ethics, setting an example for others to follow. Because of their discernment, they identified those sincere in their beliefs and those who strayed. This responsibility weighed heavily on their shoulders, but they carried it with grace and humility, always putting the needs of the community above their own.

The leaders' tireless efforts to preserve the faith have left an indelible mark on the community. Their dedication and sacrifice have ensured that the values and teachings of the faith continue to thrive, providing guidance and inspiration to all who seek spiritual enlightenment. The leaders' legacy will endure for generations to come, a testament to their unwavering commitment to preserving the faith.

And then along comes Jesus, a charismatic preacher from Nazareth, who challenges the traditions and practices of the Jewish leaders at the temple in Jerusalem. Jesus' teachings often diverge from the strict interpretations of the Old Testament laws that the religious authorities had always adhered to. His radical messages of love, forgiveness, and inclusivity shake the foundations of the established religious hierarchy, sparking controversy and debate among the people. Jesus' actions and words lead to his crucifixion, but his message of spiritual renewal and redemption continues to resonate with countless followers around the world.

People say the kingdom of heaven, as taught in the scriptures, suffers more from its nominal friends than from its most hostile opponents. This statement highlights the significance of genuine faith and devotion to the teachings of the faith. It emphasizes that faith is not merely a label or a superficial association, but a profound and personal connection to higher truths. This faith demands heartfelt experience, daily practice, and dedicated, sincere following. The message conveyed is that true faith is not just about words or appearances, but about a deep and authentic relationship with divine principles.

One needs experience to understand some parts of the Bible. Without emotion, what is human nature? It is hard, narrow, austere, and selfish. What garden can live in all its beautiful colors without the dew? We see often further through our tears than through our literary acquisitions.

Many perceive human nature, devoid of emotion, as rigid and self-centered. Emotions play a crucial role in understanding the complexities of the human psyche and behavior. Just as a garden needs dew to thrive and display its vibrant colors, humans require emotions to fully express their essence. Emotions serve as a lens through which we can perceive the world with depth and clarity, often revealing truths that go beyond mere intellectual knowledge. It is through our tears, moments of vulnerability and raw emotion, that we gain profound insights into ourselves and others.

The interplay between human nature and emotions creates a profound and intricate relationship that shapes our understanding of the world. Embracing our emotions fosters empathy and insight. This deeper understanding helps us navigate life's complexities and discover profound truths.

No person ever learns to swim by standing on the shore. The Rabbis considered their knowledge limited to the law. But there are a thousand teachers. Nature, the world, and our sweet loving mothers who teach us from birth — and along comes Jesus!

In the journey of learning and growth, wisdom and guidance come from various sources. The Rabbis, with their knowledge of the law, and the scribes, with their expertise in interpreting written texts, represent just a fraction of the myriad educators present in our lives. Nature, a nurturing force that surrounds us from birth, serves as a constant teacher, imparting valuable lessons through its cycles and interactions. And then, there is Jesus, a figure of profound teachings and compassion, who emerges as a transformative influence. Together, these diverse teachers shape our understanding and guide us through the waters of life.

In the parable of the prodigal son, we witness a powerful depiction of love, forgiveness, and reconciliation. The prodigal son, having squandered his inheritance and lived a reckless life, returns home to his father, who embraces him with open arms. The father's unconditional love and forgiveness towards his wayward son symbolize the boundless mercy and grace of God.

This parable serves as a profound illustration of how Jesus exemplifies love, mercy, and grace in his teachings and interactions with humanity. Through his life and ministry, Jesus consistently showed compassion and forgiveness to those who sought redemption and transformation. Just as the father in the parable welcomed his son back without hesitation, Jesus extends the same love and acceptance to all who come to him with a repentant heart.

The essence of this parable lies in the transformative power of love and grace over judgment and condemnation. The parable reminds us that true spirituality stems not from rigid adherence to laws and regulations, but from genuine acts of kindness, compassion, and forgiveness towards others. By embodying the love of God, we can cultivate a spirit of mercy and grace that transcends earthly boundaries and fosters deep connections with our fellow human beings.

The parable of the prodigal son inspires us to follow Jesus' example of love, mercy, and grace. May we seek to cultivate a heart that is open, forgiving, and compassionate towards all, recognizing that true fulfillment comes from embracing the divine essence of love and grace.

Today

I am writing a discourse on John 7:15 entitled "Regularities". Any insights?

John 7:15 says, "The Jews then were astonished, saying, 'How has this man become learned, having never been educated?'" This verse highlights the surprise of the Jewish leaders at Jesus' profound knowledge and wisdom despite his lack of formal education.

In exploring the theme of "Regularities," consider these angles:

Divine Wisdom vs. Human Education

Exploring Jesus' understanding of the scriptures reveals he did not learn from traditional education systems. Jesus did not gain his scriptural understanding from formal schooling or religious training; instead, his insights stemmed from divine wisdom. This unconventional source of knowledge challenges how we assume one gains wisdom and understanding. Jesus' teachings and interpretations of the scriptures serve as a testament to the transformative power of divine wisdom that transcends human education.

Breaking Social Norms: A Reflection on Jesus' Challenge to Societal Expectations

Throughout history, individuals have emerged who have defied societal norms and expectations, challenged the status quo and paved the way for change. One such prominent figure is Jesus of Nazareth, whose teachings and actions have had a profound impact on human history. Jesus' willingness to challenge established conventions and norms serves as a powerful example of how divine purpose can transcend human regularities. By examining some of the key instances in which Jesus broke social norms, we can gain insight into the transformative power of defying societal expectations.

Jesus interacted with marginalized groups, like tax collectors, Samaritans, and women, defying the social norms of his era. Jesus befriended those which society rejected. He also associated with sinners. This radical inclusivity challenged the rigid social hierarchies of his time. His famous Sermon on the Mount, in which he proclaimed blessings upon the poor, meek, and persecuted, further emphasized his commitment to uplifting the downtrodden and challenging societal norms that favored the wealthy and powerful.

Jesus' teachings on forgiveness, compassion, and love for one's enemies went against the prevailing ethic of retaliation and retribution. By advocating for a radical form of love that transcended tribal boundaries and personal grievances, Jesus challenged his followers to embody a higher moral standard that defied the logic of tit-for-tat justice. His ultimate act of sacrificial love on the cross exemplified his unwavering commitment to breaking down barriers and transforming hearts through radical acts of compassion.

Jesus' life and teachings serve as a powerful reminder that divine purpose can indeed transcend human regularities. By breaking social norms and challenging societal expectations, Jesus exemplified a radical form of love and compassion that continues to inspire people of faith and goodwill to this day. Let us, reflecting on Jesus' example, question the norms and conventions limiting our capacity for love, justice, and mercy, striving for a more inclusive and compassionate society.

Human Perception vs. Divine Reality

The Jewish leaders' astonishment serves as a poignant example of the stark contrast between human perception and divine reality. It highlights the inherent limitations of human understanding, which often hinder our ability to recognize the profound truths and regularities that exist beyond our grasp. This disparity between what we perceive and what truly is serves as a reminder of the complexities of faith and the perpetual quest for deeper spiritual insight.

In the narrative of the Jewish leaders' astonishment, we witness a powerful illustration of how our limited human perspective can obscure the divine truths that permeate the world. Despite their religious knowledge and authority, the unexpected and miraculous events that unfolded before them took aback the leaders. This serves as a cautionary tale, reminding us that our understanding is inherently flawed, unable to fully comprehend the mysteries of the divine realm.

The reaction of the Jewish leaders prompts us to reflect on the nature of faith and the challenges it presents to our perceptions. It underscores the importance of humility and open-mindedness in approaching matters of spirituality, acknowledging that our preconceived notions and biases can cloud our judgment and prevent us from truly experiencing the divine reality that surrounds us.

The story of the Jewish leaders' astonishment serves as a powerful reminder of the profound disparity between human perception and divine reality. It challenges us to question our assumptions, broaden our perspectives, and strive for a deeper understanding of the spiritual truths that shape our world. By recognizing the limitations of our own perceptions, we can cultivate a more profound appreciation for the mysteries and wonders of the divine realm.

We all need to study God's Word with more regularity!

10

A Way That Seems Right

---◆─────❈─────◆---

Proverbs 16:25: "There is a way that seemeth right unto a man, but the end thereof are the ways of death."

Life is often a journey marked by choices and decisions, each one leading us down a unique path. In our pursuit of success, happiness, and fulfillment, we constantly face options that seem right and promising. However, the ancient wisdom found in Proverbs 16:25 offers a sobering reminder: "There is a way that appears to be right, but in the end, it leads to death." This verse challenges us to question our assumptions, examine our motives, and seek guidance beyond our limited understanding. In this discourse, we will delve into the profound implications of this proverb, exploring its relevance to our everyday lives and the importance of aligning our paths with divine wisdom.

This passage offers profound theological insights into human judgment and divine wisdom. It underscores the limitations of human understanding and the potential dangers of relying solely on our own perceptions and instincts.

1. Human Fallibility: Theologically, this proverb highlights the concept of human fallibility. It suggests that their own limited perspective can often deceive human beings. This aligns with the biblical theme of human imperfection and the need for divine guidance. In the Christian tradition, passages such as Isaiah 55:8-9 echo this idea; God declares, "For my thoughts are not your thoughts, neither are your ways my ways."

2. The Consequences of Sin: This verse also points to the consequences of sin and disobedience. We can see the "way that appears to be right" as a metaphor for paths leading away from God's will. Christian theology often describes sin as a deviation from God's intended path,

leading to spiritual death. Romans 6:23 supports this interpretation, which states, "For the wages of sin is death, but the gift of God is eternal life in Christ Jesus our Lord."

3. The Necessity of Divine Wisdom: Proverbs 16:25 emphasizes the necessity of seeking divine wisdom and guidance. Theologically, it reinforces the idea that true wisdom comes from God and that human understanding is insufficient without His direction. This is a central theme in the book of Proverbs, as seen in Proverbs 3:5-6: "Trust in the Lord with all thine heart and lean not unto thine own understanding; in all thy ways submit to him, and he will make thy paths straight."

4. The Role of Faith: Faith plays a crucial role in navigating life's choices. This verse encourages believers to place their trust in God rather than their own judgment. In Christian theology, faith is a means of aligning one's life with God's will, leading to spiritual growth and eternal life.

5. Redemptive Hope: While the verse warns of the dangers of misguided paths, it also implicitly offers hope. Through faith in Jesus Christ and adherence to God's wisdom, believers can avoid the pitfalls of deceptive paths and find genuine life. This redemptive hope is central to

the Christian message and underscores the transformative power of divine grace.

This theological view can provide a deeper understanding of Proverbs 16:25 and its significance in the Christian faith.

Have you ever made a decision that seemed right at the time but led to unexpected consequences? I am quite certain that we all have.

A distant city offered Paul a lucrative job. The job, with its higher salary, better position, and prestigious company, appeared to be the perfect opportunity. Fueled by excitement, Paul swiftly accepted the offer without delving into other crucial factors. However, upon relocating to the new city, Paul encountered unforeseen challenges. The soaring cost of living, poor work-life balance, and unsupportive environment were stark contrasts to his expectations. Paul grappled with stress, loneliness, and a sense of dissatisfaction, missing the sense of community and connections he had left behind.

This narrative reflects the timeless wisdom found in Proverbs 16:25, emphasizing the need to look beyond surface-level appearances and carefully weigh all aspects before deciding. It serves as a poignant reminder that the right path may lead to unexpected consequences if not approached with prudence and discernment. Paul's experience underscores the significance of thoughtful decision-making and seeking guidance to navigate through life's opportunities and challenges.

A rich history of theological interpretation surrounds Proverbs 16:25, and we have gathered noteworthy quotes from some of our earliest theological thinkers.

Quote by Augustine of Hippo: "Human pride and self-reliance often lead us astray. It is only through humility and seeking God's wisdom that we can find the true path to life."

Augustine of Hippo, a renowned theologian and philosopher, emphasized the detrimental effects of human pride and self-reliance. According to him, these qualities can blind us to the truth and lead us astray from the path of righteousness. Augustine believed humility and a sincere search for God's wisdom bring true wisdom and guidance.

In a world filled with distractions and temptations, Augustine's teachings remind us of the importance of humility and seeking divine guidance. By acknowledging our limitations and surrendering to a higher power, we can navigate life's challenges with clarity and purpose. It is through humility and a willingness to seek God's wisdom that we can find true fulfillment and meaning in our lives.

Thomas Aquinas once stated, "The way that seems right to a man is often the way of self-will and disobedience to God's law. True wisdom lies in aligning our will with the divine will." This profound statement highlights the importance of humility and submission to a higher authority in achieving true wisdom. Aquinas emphasizes the need to set aside personal desires and ambitions to follow the path ordained by God.

John Chrysostom also noted the deceptive nature of human perception. He stated, "The path that appears right to man is often paved with the desires of the flesh and the deceit of the world."

Both Aquinas and Chrysostom underscore the significance of aligning one's will with the divine will as the key to attaining true wisdom. By recognizing the limitations of human understanding and embracing a life guided by faith and obedience, individuals can navigate through the complexities of life with clarity and purpose.

Wesley's journey serves as a cautionary tale about the dangers of overconfidence. Wesley, a high school standout, approached college entrance exams with a sense of assurance in his abilities. Believing that his innate intelligence and prior successes would suffice, he neglected to dedicate considerable time to studying for the exams. However, when Wesley received his results, a harsh reality confronted him—his scores fell short of his expectations. The discrepancy between his expected outcome and the actual results served as a wake-up call for Wesley. He had misjudged the level of preparation required and overestimated his own capabilities.

This narrative underscores the importance of humility and diligence in the pursuit of goals. Wesley's reliance on past achievements as a sole indicator of future success proved to be a misguided approach. It serves as a reminder that genuine progress demands a willingness to seek guidance, put in the effort, and continually challenge oneself. By acknowledging the limitations of overconfidence and embracing a mindset of continuous growth, individuals can navigate challenges with resilience and adaptability. Wesley's story serves as a poignant reminder of the perils of complacency and the transformative power of humility in the face of adversity.

Considering this, remember that we don't receive wisdom in abundance without effort, but gain it through diligence and learning from others. It is often the result of hard work and dedication.

11

Determined to Succeed

JEREMIAH 29:11

As a child, I never let someone telling me I couldn't do it stop me. I was incredibly determined and would always set my focus on achieving whatever goal I needed. This unwavering determination became a defining trait of my character. Whether it was learning a new skill, overcoming a challenge, or pursuing a dream, I approached every situation with a mindset of perseverance and flexibility. This attitude not only helped me achieve my goals but also shaped me into the person I am today.

I passionately believe determination and hard work can overcome any obstacle and turn any dream into reality.

Carmen, a determined young woman, grew up in a financially struggling family but harbored big dreams of becoming a doctor to provide medical assistance to those in need. Her motivation stemmed from witnessing various traumatic events within her family where the lack of insurance prevented them from accessing necessary medical care.

Despite facing financial constraints, Carmen's family wholeheartedly supported her aspirations, although they could not provide her with the financial means to pursue her dreams. Carmen's unwavering determination and desire to make a difference in the lives of others served as the driving force behind her pursuit of a career in medicine.

Carmen was always an excellent student and scored top grades on every subject. In high school, she had to balance her schoolwork with part-time jobs to help the family. She stayed up most nights until late, studying for the next day's exams. Her only light came from a kerosene lamp.

Scripture Inspiration: *"I can do all things through Christ who strengthens me." - Philippians 4:13*

This verse was a source of comfort for Carmen during her toughest times. Whenever she felt overwhelmed, she remembered that her strength came from a higher power. Carmen found solace in the words of this verse, drawing strength and courage from the belief that there was a greater force guiding her through challenges. In moments of doubt and despair, she held onto the faith that she was not alone in her struggles. This verse served as a constant reminder for Carmen to trust in something beyond herself and to find peace amid adversity.

Carmen's resilience shone through as she navigated her family's financial challenges, eventually earning a scholarship to a local university. Despite this achievement, she faced a heavy workload and intense pressure to excel in her studies. The struggle became especially daunting when she encountered a challenging anatomy exam one day. In moments of doubt, she found solace in the scripture from Joshua 1:9, which reminded her to be strong, courageous, and to trust in the presence of the Lord. Carmen's journey is a testament to her perseverance and faith in overcoming obstacles on her path to success.

This scripture served as Carmen's beacon of hope. On the eve of her exam, she prayed and reminded herself of these words, finding the courage to continue studying and passing with excellence.

The busy hospital, with its long hours and emotionally taxing cases, truly tested Carmen's faith during her medical school internship. The challenging environment often left her feeling drained, but one case of a young boy with a rare illness hit her especially hard. Carmen faced difficulties, but she held onto Galatians 6:9: "And let us not be weary in well doing: for in due season we shall reap, if we faint not.." She believed her hard work would pay off.

Her relentless determination paid off as she played a crucial role in the young boy's recovery, earning the respect and admiration of her peers. Carmen's experience during her internship serves as a powerful reminder of the importance of faith, determination, and resolute commitment in the face of adversity.

After years of unswerving determination, Carmen finally graduated from medical school, ready to embark on her career as a doctor. Her journey was a testament to the power of perseverance, faith, and the belief that no dream is too big if you have the determination to pursue it.

Carmen's path to becoming a doctor was difficult. She faced numerous challenges, from rigorous academic requirements to demanding clinical rotations. Despite setbacks and moments of doubt, Carmen never wavered in her commitment to her goal. She spent countless hours studying, sacrificing social events and personal time to excel in her coursework.

Along the way, she found support from mentors, friends, and family members who believed in her and encouraged her to keep pushing forward. Carmen's journey to becoming a doctor taught her perseverance, faith, and the power of hard work. Now, in her white coat, she knows she can achieve any dream. Carmen's story serves as an inspiration to all who dare to dream big and pursue their passions with unwavering dedication.

Jeremiah 29:11

"For I know the thoughts that I think toward you, saith the Lord, thoughts of peace, and not of evil, to give you an expected end."

This verse from the book of Jeremiah is a powerful reminder of God's love and care for His people. It reassures us that God has a specific plan for each of us, a plan that brings us prosperity, hope, and a bright future. By trusting in God's plans and surrendering to His will, we can find comfort and assurance that He is always working for our good.

Determination can be a powerful force that drives individuals to overcome challenges and achieve remarkable success. Here are a few inspiring examples of determination across different fields that serve as testaments to the human spirit and resilience.

Helen Keller:

Despite losing her sight and hearing at an early age, Helen Keller defied all odds to become the first deaf-blind person to earn a Bachelor of Arts degree. She became a renowned author, political activist, and lecturer, inspiring generations with her perseverance and achievements.

Thomas Edison:

Known for his invention of the electric light bulb, Thomas Edison faced numerous failures and setbacks before finally succeeding. His unwavering determination and persistence were instrumental in his groundbreaking innovations that revolutionized the world.

J. K. Rowling:

The journey of J. K. Rowling, author of the beloved Harry Potter series, is a testament to the power of determination. Despite facing multiple rejections from publishers, Rowling persisted in sharing her magical world with the world, eventually achieving global acclaim and inspiring millions of readers.

Bethany Hamilton:

Professional surfer Bethany Hamilton displayed extraordinary determination and courage after losing her arm in a shark attack. Just one month later, she returned to surfing, continuing to compete with and inspiring others with her resilience and positive attitude in the face of adversity.

Nelson Mandela:

Imprisoned for 27 years for his fight against apartheid in South Africa, Nelson Mandela never lost sight of his commitment to justice and equality. His unwavering determination led him to become the country's first black president, symbolizing peace and reconciliation worldwide.

Malala Yousafzai:

Despite facing life-threatening violence for advocating for girls' education in Pakistan, Malala Yousafzai's unwavering determination and courage have made her a global icon for education and women's rights. Her resilience and advocacy earned her the title of the youngest-ever Nobel Prize laureate.

These inspiring stories show the transformative power of determination, showing how it can lead to incredible achievements and inspire others to overcome obstacles in pursuit of their dreams. Each of these individuals serves as a beacon of hope and resilience, reminding us that with determination, anything is possible.

In today's challenging world, numerous individuals, like Carmen, might face considerable difficulties in their lives, struggling to cope and overcome obstacles. Take a moment out of your day to speak kindly to them, and may God bless you throughout your journey.

12

The Stetson Effect

In the heart of bustling cities and remote villages alike, the sight of a weathered Stetson hat had become a beacon of hope and guidance for countless mission trip teams. As a team leader, I oversaw every project. My leadership was steady and reassuring.

Jeremiah 29:11 has often been a source of comfort and guidance for me as a leader: "For I know the plans I have for you... plans to prosper you and not to harm you, plans to give you hope and a future."

Each mission trip was a new adventure, filled with challenges, uncertainties, and opportunities for growth. My role was to navigate these waters, to inspire and guide my team through the unknown. The Stetson became more than just a hat; it was a symbol of our unity and my commitment to their safety and success.

In crowded airports where the noise and chaos threatened to overwhelm, the sight of the Stetson cutting through the sea of travelers reassured my team. It was a constant reminder that they were not alone and that their leader was always within reach. In city squares, where the unfamiliar surroundings could easily disorient, the hat became a lighthouse, guiding them back to the safe harbor of our group.

Psalm 23:4 resonated deeply during challenging times: "Even though I walk through the valley of the shadow of death, I will fear no evil, for thou art with me." My leadership, symbolized by my hat, helped team members reconnect.

One trip to a bustling city in South America stood out. We had arrived at a sprawling market, the vibrant colors and cacophony of sounds creating a sensory overload. As we navigated through the maze of stalls, a sudden realization hit me—one of our team members was missing. Panic threatened to take hold, but I knew I had to remain calm for the sake of the others.

I climbed onto a low wall, raising the Stetson high above the crowd. Within moments, I saw a relieved face pushing through the throng of people, eyes locked on the hat that signaled their way back. The joy and relief in that moment were palpable, and it reinforced the importance of the hat and my role as a leader.

Throughout our mission trips, the Stetson served as a constant reminder of the responsibilities and trust placed upon me. It was a symbol of the guidance, protection, and determination that leadership demands. I often drew strength from Proverbs 3:5-6: "Trust in the Lord with all your heart and lean not on your own understanding; in all your ways submit to him, and he will make your paths straight."

As our journeys continued, the Stetson hat bore witness to countless stories of perseverance, camaraderie, and growth. It became a cherished emblem of our shared experiences and the unwavering dedication that leadership entails.

My faded brown hat now sits on the hatrack inside our front door. I am retired now and will often gaze up at it and hear it softly whisper, "Are you ready to go again?"

Individuals from diverse backgrounds show leadership in many ways. A specific role or position does not limit leadership; rather, anyone who inspires, motivates, and guides others toward a common goal exhibits this quality. Various settings, including workplaces, community organizations, sports teams, and educational institutions, demonstrate effective leadership. It involves traits such as communication, empathy, decisiveness, and the ability to inspire trust and respect. Overall, leadership is about influencing and empowering others to achieve success and make a positive impact in their respective environments.

I learned as a leader that my job was to lead, not to do all the work. It was hard to do this task, for I always aspired to be involved in the actual work we were doing. However, someone had to prepare, plan, and oversee the work. That's where I found my place with each team.

Here are some insightful quotes from notable individuals on the theme of leadership:

John C. Maxwell: "A leader is one who knows the way, goes the way, and shows the way."

Lao Tzu: "A leader is best when people barely know he exists. When his work is done, his aim fulfilled, they will say, We did it ourselves."

Mahatma Gandhi: "The best way to find yourself is to lose yourself in the service of others."

Peter Drucker: "The leader of the past knew how to tell. The leader of the future knows how to ask."

Nelson Mandela: "It is better to lead from behind and to put others in front, especially when you celebrate victory when nice things occur. You take the front line when there is danger. Then people will appreciate your leadership."

Simon Sinek: "Leaders are not responsible for the job. They are responsible for the people who are responsible for the job."

Rosalynn Carter: "A leader takes people where they want to go. A great leader takes people where they don't necessarily want to go, but ought to be."

John Quincy Adams: "If your actions inspire others to dream more, learn more, do more, and become more, you are a leader."

Steve Jobs: "Innovation distinguishes between a leader and a follower."

Dwight D. Eisenhower: "Leadership is the art of getting someone else to do something you want done because he wants to do it."

Team members' comments like, "Thanks for leading us" or "We appreciate you being there" always delighted me at the end of our trips. It reinforced the importance of building strong relationships and fostering a sense of teamwork within the group. As a leader, I strive to cultivate an environment where team members feel valued and supported, recognizing the significance of everyone's contributions.

When reflecting on my leadership style, my strength lies in my ability to communicate effectively and empathize with others. I am a firm believer in open and honest communication, ensuring that team members feel heard and understood. By fostering a culture of transparency and trust, I can create a supportive and collaborative environment where everyone feels empowered to voice their opinions and ideas.

I excel in problem-solving and decision-making, using a combination of analytical thinking and creative solutions to navigate challenges effectively. I am adept at delegating tasks based on individual strengths and skills, maximizing the team's potential, and achieving our goals efficiently.

Overall, I root my leadership style in appreciation, communication, and collaboration. I prioritize building strong relationships with my team members and empowering them to succeed. By leveraging my strengths in communication, problem-solving, and empathy, I strive to create a positive and productive work environment where everyone can thrive and contribute to our collective success. I call it "The Stetson Effect."

13

Tapestries of Hope

A devastating tornado struck Cedar Ridge last May, carving a two-mile-wide path of destruction. The tornado's impact caused significant property damage and loss of life. Tragically, the community mourned the loss of six residents, including a six-month-old child. The aftermath of the tornado left a profound impact on the tight-knit community of Cedar Ridge, highlighting the importance of resilience and support in times of crisis.

Sweeping through Cedar Ridge, the tornado left a trail of devastation with its destructive force. The tornado destroyed homes, uprooted trees, and damaged infrastructure. The sudden and overwhelming destruction left the community reeling, struggling to cope with the loss of life and widespread damage.

Losing six residents, including a young child, served as a stark reminder of the fragility of life and the indiscriminate nature of natural disasters. The community came together in grief, offering support and solace to those who had lost loved ones. The tragedy brought into focus the resilience of the community, as neighbors banded together to help rebuild and recover from the disaster.

In the days and weeks following the tornado, Cedar Ridge rallied around those affected, providing assistance, shelter, and emotional support. The outpouring of compassion and solidarity showed the strength of the community in the face of adversity. Through collective efforts and steadfast determination, Cedar Ridge began the lengthy process of rebuilding and healing.

The devastating tornado that struck Cedar Ridge last May had a profound impact on the community, highlighting the importance of resilience and support in times of crisis. Despite the loss and destruction, the spirit of Cedar Ridge remained unbroken as neighbors came together to support one another and rebuild their lives. The tragedy served as a reminder of the strength and unity that can emerge in the face of adversity, highlighting the power of the community in times of need.

Martha, a single mother who tragically lost her home in a disaster, faced the daunting task of providing for her 5-year-old son amidst the chaos. Struggling to make ends meet and rebuild their lives, Martha's situation seemed dire. However, in a heartwarming turn of events, Henry Johnson, a retired military veteran grappling with loneliness, extended a helping hand to Martha and her son.

Moved by compassion and a sense of duty, Henry welcomed them into his home, offering them a haven until Martha could have her own home rebuilt. This act of kindness offered Martha, and her son shelter and forged a supportive friendship between previously unconnected people. Amid adversity, this story serves as a shining example of the power of empathy and human connection in times of need.

Pastor Ronnie, a dedicated leader in the community and his local congregation, worked tirelessly to support the people of Cedar Ridge during challenging times. Despite feeling overwhelmed, he remained resolute in his commitment to be a steadfast pillar of faith for the community. The recent devastation at Cedar Ridge Elementary School shook the town, but Principal Carter's determination to rebuild and provide stability for the children showed steadfast strength and resilience. Together, Pastor Ronnie and Principal Carter exemplified the spirit of unity and hope in Cedar Ridge during times of adversity.

A devastating tragedy struck their small town. Through their faith, the residents united to rebuild their community. Dealing with their own personal losses and challenges, their unwavering faith and determination united them to rebuild. Amidst the destruction, the local church, led by Pastor Ronnie, opened its doors. It offered hope and a place for the community to unite, discuss support, and plan the town's rebuilding.

The community was willing to help, even though they knew it would require sacrifice from everyone. Their collective efforts and shared faith created a strong bond that propelled them forward in their mission to rebuild and heal. As they worked side by side, the community found solace in each other's company, finding strength in unity and resilience in their shared beliefs.

Through their collaboration and mutual support, the community saw signs of progress and hope. Each small step towards restoration was a testament to the power of faith and community coming together in times of adversity. The community, once shattered, rebuilt. Their tireless work, unshakable faith, and determination fueled their progress toward a common goal.

In times of crisis, individuals like Mr. Johnson, Pastor Ronnie, and Ms. Carter steps up to lead their community towards recovery and renewal. Mr. Johnson, with his expertise in coordinating rescue missions, ensures that those in distress receive the help they need promptly. Meanwhile, Pastor Ronnie dedicates himself to providing spiritual and emotional support to those grappling with the aftermath of the disaster. Ms. Carter, as the principal of the local elementary school, mobilizes volunteers to aid in the reconstruction efforts, symbolizing a beacon of hope for the students and their families.

As these remarkable individuals unite their efforts, a spirit of solidarity and compassion emerges within the community. Neighbors come together to rebuild homes, sharing resources, and offer solace to one another. The collective acts of kindness and generosity form a tapestry of hope, weaving a narrative of resilience and unity in the face of adversity. The church, under Pastor Ronnie's guidance, transforms into a sanctuary of refuge and optimism, providing a safe space for community members to find solace and strength.

Amid chaos and destruction, the unwavering dedication of volunteers highlights the resilience of communities facing adversity. Their collaborative efforts go beyond providing practical assistance; they create a sense of belonging and support for those affected. These selfless actions serve as a beacon of hope, inspiring others to come together and work towards a better future. The volunteers' commitment highlights that in times of need, it is the collective spirit of compassion and cooperation that sustains and uplifts us all.

Amid the struggles, moments of divine intervention and breakthroughs occur. For instance, a supply truck carrying much-needed resources arrives just in time before the rains hit, providing essential aid to the community.

As the community slowly rebuilds, the community holds a special service to express gratitude for the support and miracles experienced. Each individual shares their faith and unity through the shared experience of overcoming disaster. This document encapsulates the power of community resilience and the profound impact of coming together in times of crisis.

The story of Cedar Ridge reaches a poignant conclusion, leaving readers with a sense of hope and unity. Emerging stronger and more united, the community overcame trials and challenges. The characters within the narrative have undergone profound growth, deepening their faith and resilience in the face of adversity. Their individual journeys intricately woven together form a tapestry of lives that stand as a testament to God's providence and unwavering care. Through the highs and lows, the story beautifully illustrates the power of faith and the resilience of the human spirit.

14

Human Praise vs. God's Praise

P raise is an expression that involves giving positive feedback or admiration to someone for their actions, achievements, qualities, or behavior. It is a way of acknowledging and appreciating the efforts and accomplishments of others. Praise can come in various forms, such as verbal compliments, written notes, public recognition, or gestures of appreciation. It serves as a powerful motivator, boosting confidence and self-esteem and strengthening relationships. Effective praise is specific, genuine, and tailored to the individual, highlighting the unique aspects that deserve recognition.

When we consider praise, I am drawn to the comparison between human praise versus God's praise. Praise is a fundamental aspect of human interaction, expressing admiration, gratitude, and recognition for others. Human praise is often based on subjective judgments and subjective opinions, influenced by factors such as culture, upbringing, and individual preferences.

God's praise is pure, unconditional, and transcendent. It is based on divine wisdom and righteousness, reflecting the perfection and holiness of God. The comparison between human praise and God's praise offers insights into relationships, values, and beliefs that shape our understanding of praise in different contexts.

When we succeed, family, friends, and associates often complement our achievements, adding to our praise. This form may come in positive or negative ways.

If we seek praise for a skillful trick that we have performed, then the praise we receive is not genuine praise. Even when we achieve remarkable things and consider them successful accomplishments, it's not always clear that God views these accomplishments as genuine praise.

In human society, there is a tendency to admire and applaud things that are fast and immediate. Whether it solves a problem or instant success, we often prioritize and celebrate swift results. Various aspects of our lives, from technology to entertainment, reveal this preference for immediacy. However, it is important to consider the implications of this culture of instant gratification and the impact it has on individuals and society.

Society commonly idolizes individuals who amass wealth, sometimes at the expense of others deprived of their resources. This dynamic reveals a deeper cultural problem: we prioritize success and wealth over ethics and the well-being of others. The glorification of those who accumulate riches without regard for the impact on others highlights a systemic problem of inequality and exploitation. Critically examining these power dynamics and challenging the notion that success achieved through the detriment of others is worthy of admiration or respect is important.

As the salaries of sports figures continue to skyrocket, reaching astronomical figures such as $100 million per year, my enthusiasm for sporting events has waned. It is disheartening to see athletes demanding such exorbitant sums, leading me to question the value and worthiness of their contributions. While their skills and achievements may be impressive, the disparity between their earnings and those of average individuals is staggering. This trend has left me feeling disillusioned and reluctant to support or praise these athletes who command such excessive salaries. It raises important questions about the priorities and values within the world of sports and the broader society.

Considering all this, the Bible offers straightforward answers about those God praises. Let's take a look.

Matthew 18:3, Jesus says, "Verily I say unto you, except ye be converted, and become as little children, ye shall not enter into the kingdom of heaven." It emphasizes the importance of humility, innocence, and open heartedness, like that of a child, in spiritual growth and acceptance.

In the pursuit of a meaningful existence, it is crucial to maintain a sense of wonder and purity. This involves shifting the focus from material wealth and societal success to embracing humility and childlike innocence.

Jesus often highlighted the importance of simplicity and purity of the heart, emphasizing the value of childlike faith. In the Bible, he praised little children and emphasized that to inherit the kingdom of heaven, one must embody the qualities of a child.

A man humbly sought God's mercy at the temple, acknowledging his flaws. This story highlights humility and repentance's importance in spiritual growth. This narrative encourages individuals to approach life with a humble and open heart, ready to embrace wonder and purity in all aspects of their journey.

The story references the Parable of the Pharisee and the Tax Collector from Luke 18:9–14. In this story, Jesus contrasts the attitudes of two men who go to the temple to pray. The Pharisee boasts about his righteousness, while the tax collector humbly acknowledges his sinfulness and pleads for God's mercy by saying, "God, be merciful to me, a sinner."

This parable highlights the importance of humility, repentance, and recognizing our need for God's grace rather than relying on self-righteousness.

In the biblical accounts found in Mark 12:41–44 and Luke 21:1-4, we learn of the poignant narrative known as the Widow's Offering. As Jesus sits near the temple treasury, observing the act of giving, he witnesses a display of generosity from various individuals. Among them are wealthy donors who contribute significant sums of money. However, the scene takes a profound turn when a poor widow approaches and quietly places two small copper coins, or mites, into the treasury.

Jesus, recognizing the true essence of giving, calls his disciples to attention and shares a timeless lesson. He commends the widow's offering as surpassing the others in value, despite its meager appearance. The widow's sacrificial gift, given out of poverty, resonates deeply with Jesus. He emphasizes that her contribution, though small in monetary terms, holds far greater significance because of the spirit of selflessness and faith behind it.

This story serves as a powerful reminder of the principles of generosity, humility, and faith. This story challenges us to consider not just the quantity of our gifts but the sincerity and sacrifice behind giving them. The Widow's Offering stands as a testament to the profound impact of genuine giving, inspiring us to reflect on the motives and intentions behind our own acts of charity.

In the Bible, there are numerous individuals who have received God's blessings and praises. While the list is extensive, the common thread among them is their meekness, humility, contriteness, and their recognition of their neediness before God. These characteristics have earned them the praise of the Lord, highlighting His favor towards those who embody such virtues.

1. **Abraham**: Known as the father of faith, Abraham displayed unwavering trust in God's promises, even when faced with insurmountable challenges. His obedience and faithfulness led to God blessing him abundantly.

2. **Ruth**: A Moabite woman who exemplified loyalty and selflessness towards her mother-in-law, Naomi. Ruth's humility and dedication caught the attention of Boaz, who eventually became her husband. Through her faithfulness, God blessed Ruth.

3. **David**: People described King David as a man after God's own heart, despite his flaws and shortcomings. His sincere repentance and genuine worship led him to God, who blessed him with victories in battle and a legacy.

The examples of Abraham, Ruth, and David serve as reminders of God's preference for those who possess qualities of meekness, humility, contriteness, and neediness. By acknowledging our dependence on God and approaching Him with a humble heart, we open ourselves up to His blessings and praises, just as these biblical figures did.

Matthew 25:35-40:

*"For **I was hungry** and you gave me something to eat; **I was thirsty** and you gave me something to drink; **I was a stranger** and you invited me in; **I needed clothes** and you clothed me; **I was sick** and you looked after me; **I was in prison** and you came to visit me."*

This passage is part of a larger parable where Jesus speaks about the Final Judgment, emphasizing the importance of showing compassion and kindness to others. To these, Jesus entrusts the kingdom of heaven.

May our goal in life be to show that same compassion and kindness to those around us. God bless you on your journey today.

15

The Silver-Tongued Orator

MARK 7:6-7

I n the picturesque village of Simpson, nestled amidst serene rolling hills and towering ancient oaks, lived a young man named Bill. Known throughout the village for his eloquence and charm, Bill possessed a unique gift of speaking with a silver tongue, enchanting all who had the enjoyment of listening to him. His words were like an intricately woven tapestry that captured the hearts and minds of those around him.

One fateful day, the village elders gave Bill the prestigious task of delivering the opening speech for the annual Harvest Festival. This cherished tradition brought
the tight-knit community together in jubilant celebration
and heartfelt gratitude. With humility and gratitude, Bill
accepted this honor and dedicated himself to crafting a
speech that would resonate with the villagers.

As Bill sat by the babbling brook, seeking inspiration
for his speech, an elderly traveler approached him. The
traveler's eyes held a profound wisdom that only time and
life experiences could give. Turning to Bill, the traveler
posed a thought-provoking question, inquiring whether
Bill's actions mirrored the sincerity and grace of his speech.

Taken aback by the traveler's inquiry, Bill reflected on
his response. After a moment of contemplation, he replied
with conviction, expressing his belief that his actions indeed reflected the same sincerity and integrity as his words.

Intrigued by the traveler's question, Bill asked why. He
wanted a conversation that would challenge his views and
broaden his understanding. The traveler sighed and recited a passage Bill had often heard but never understood:
"'These people honor me with their lips, but their hearts

are far from me. They worship me in vain; their teachings are merely human rules.'"

The words struck a chord within Bill. He realized that while he could eloquently express gratitude and praise, his actions often fell short of the ideals he spoke of. His words were like the fall leaves—beautiful but fleeting, easily scattered by the wind. The traveler continued, "True honor comes not from the lips but from the heart. Let your actions speak louder than your words, and your life will be a testament to your sincerity."

This encounter with the traveler served as a wake-up call for Bill, prompting him to reevaluate the way he conducted himself in his daily life. It made him realize the importance of aligning his words with his actions and ensuring that his deeds reflected the values and beliefs he professed.

From that day on, Bill attempted to let his actions speak for him, to let the sincerity in his heart shine through in all that he did. The traveler's words became a guiding light, a reminder that true integrity lies not in what we say but in what we do. And as Bill embarked on this journey of self-discovery and growth, he found that his life became richer, more meaningful, and more in harmony with his true self.

Bill nodded, a newfound resolve taking root within him. He knew he had to change to align his actions with the words he so effortlessly spoke. As the Harvest Festival approached, Bill tirelessly helped the villagers prepare, offering his support wherever needed.

As the days passed, Bill's commitment to living authentically deepened. He actively sought opportunities to show his values through his actions, whether it was assisting an elderly neighbor with household chores or volunteering at the local community center. The transformation within Bill was clear to those around him, as his integrity and sincerity shone through in all aspects of his life. The Harvest Festival became a symbol of his newfound dedication to living with purpose and meaning, as he worked tirelessly to ensure its success, embodying the values he held dear.

Bill's journey of self-discovery and growth was a life-changing experience filled with challenges and moments of clarity. Each obstacle he encountered became an opportunity for him to strengthen his resolve to live with integrity and authenticity. The encounter with the traveler marked a significant turning point in his life, sparking positive change and setting him on a path towards a more fulfilling and harmonious existence.

As Bill navigated through the difficulties of his journey, he found solace in the newfound sense of purpose and direction that emerged from his interactions with the traveler. Their words of wisdom resonated deeply with him, serving as a guiding light through the darkness of uncertainty. With each step forward, Bill felt a growing sense of confidence in his ability to overcome obstacles and embrace the challenges that lay ahead.

Looking towards the future, Bill embraced the knowledge that he was on the right track, fueled by his own integrity and the profound impact of the traveler's insights. He emerged from his experiences as a more resilient and self-aware person. He's now prepared to meet any challenge with grace and determination.

Bill's journey of self-discovery and growth had not been easy, but it had been incredibly rewarding. Through perseverance and introspection, he had unlocked a newfound sense of purpose and authenticity that would guide him towards a more fulfilling and harmonious existence. As he continued his path, Bill carried with him the lessons learned from the traveler, forever grateful for the role they had played in shaping his transformative journey.

When the day of the festival arrived, Bill stood before the crowd, his heart aligned with his words. He spoke of unity, kindness, and genuine gratitude. This time, his speech was not just a string of eloquent phrases, but a reflection of the man he had become.

As the annual festival in the village of Simpson ended, a sense of admiration and respect filled the air. The villagers, who had witnessed Bill's actions throughout the event, now looked at him with newfound respect. Bill's unwavering commitment to living by the values he preached had not gone unnoticed. Even the elderly traveler, who had been observing from the edge of the crowd, smiled knowingly at the sight before him. Bill had utterly understood the essence of honor and sincerity.

Through his actions and behavior during the festival, Bill had undergone a transformation that would leave a lasting impact on the village of Simpson. The villagers now saw him as a man of integrity and principle, someone who embodied the values that they held dear. His newfound understanding of honor and sincerity had not only enriched his own life but had also brought a sense of unity and inspiration to the community.

As the sun set on the festival grounds, the villagers gathered around Bill, expressing their gratitude and admiration for the positive influence he had brought to their village. The elderly traveler, now standing among them, nodded approvingly. Bill's journey of self-discovery and personal growth touched the hearts of those around him and left a lasting legacy.

16

The Timekeeper's Daughter

In the small, forgotten village of Ellenwood lived an old clockmaker named Timothy. Known for his impeccable craftsmanship, Timothy's clocks weren't merely instruments for telling time; they were works of art, each possessing a piece of his soul. But the most remarkable of all his creations was the grand town clock that stood in the village square, towering over the cobblestone streets. Timothy had a daughter named Lara, a bright and curious girl who spent her days in her father's workshop, learning the secrets of the trade. She had inherited her father's talent and passion for clockmaking, and it wasn't long before she made her own clocks, each more beautiful and intricate than the last.

Timothy's workshop was a haven of creativity and innovation, filled with the soothing sound of ticking clocks and the scent of wood shavings. Lara would spend hours by her father's side, observing his meticulous work and absorbing his wisdom. As she grew older, her skills blossomed, and she experimented with new techniques and designs, pushing the boundaries of traditional clockmaking.

The grand town clock in the village square was a symbol of Timothy's legacy, a testament to his dedication and artistry. People from everywhere would come to marvel at its intricate mechanisms and exquisite details. Lara often stood by its towering presence, feeling a deep sense of pride and responsibility to carry on her father's legacy.

As the years passed, Lara's clocks gained recognition beyond Ellenwood. Collectors and enthusiasts, each piece a masterpiece of precision and beauty, sought after her creations. Ellenwood, a once-forgotten village, gained fame as the home of Lara, a talented clockmaker carrying on her father Timothy's generation-old legacy.

One stormy night, a mysterious traveler arrived at Timothy's workshop. Cloaked in shadows, he introduced himself as Lord Randall, a collector of rare and unique timepieces. He had heard of Timothy's prowess and came with an unusual request. "I seek a clock that does not just measure time but controls it," Lord Randall said, his eyes gleaming with an otherworldly light. Timothy hesitated, for he had heard tales of such clocks—ones that could twist the very fabric of time. But the traveler offered a fortune beyond imagination, enough to secure Lara's future and the village's prosperity.

As the wind howled outside, Timothy contemplated the risks and rewards of creating such a powerful timepiece. The village desperately needed resources, and Lara, his daughter, dreamed of a better life beyond their humble abode. Lord Randall's offer seemed like a once-in-a-lifetime opportunity, but the implications of manipulating time itself weighed heavily on Timothy's conscience.

Despite his reservations, the allure of wealth and security for his loved ones proved too strong to resist. With a heavy heart, Timothy agreed to take on the challenge of crafting the legendary clock for Lord Randall. Little did he know that his decision would set off a chain of events that would test the very fabric of reality itself.

The workshop buzzed with activity as Timothy delved into the intricate task of creating a clock unlike any other. He imbued each cog and gear with a power transcending mere mechanics. As the days turned into weeks, Timothy's unease grew, overshadowed by a sense of foreboding that loomed over the project.

As the last pieces fell into place, a sense of dread settled upon Timothy. The clock stood before him, a masterpiece of craftsmanship and dark magic intertwined. Lord Randall's eyes gleamed with triumph as he took possession of the time-controlling clock. The village rejoiced at the newfound wealth and prosperity that flowed from the mysterious timepiece.

In the small village nestled among rolling hills, Timothy, the skilled clockmaker, embarked on a daring project to create a clock that could control time itself. Driven by a thirst for knowledge and power, Timothy poured his heart and soul into his creation, oblivious to the consequences that lay ahead.

But as days turned into nights and the clock's influence spread, whispers of anomalies and disturbances in the fabric of time surfaced. Reality itself seemed to warp and twist around the village, casting any doubt and fear over Timothy's creation. Now, faced with the consequences of his decision, Timothy must grapple with the genuine cost of tampering with the forces of time. Will he be able to undo the havoc wreaked by the time-controlling clock, or will he be forever bound by the consequences of his actions? Only time will tell.

With a heavy heart, Timothy agreed and worked on the most ambitious clock he had ever created. For months, he toiled away, his hands never resting, guided by ancient tomes and forbidden knowledge. Lara watched in awe and concern as her father grew more obsessed and frailer with each passing day.

The Enigmatic Clock

The clock, a magnificent creation adorned with intricate symbols and mysterious runes, was finally complete. Lord Randall, the benefactor who had commissioned its construction, returned to claim his prize as promised. In exchange, he left behind a chest of gold, fulfilling his end of the bargain. However, as he departed, a sinister smile lingered on his lips, casting a shadow of unease over Lara, the clockmaker.

Unable to shake the feeling of dread that enveloped her, Lara delved deep into her late father's notes, seeking to unravel the enigma surrounding the clock. Days turned into nights as she meticulously studied the intricate workings and ancient designs of the timepiece. Then, one fateful evening as the village basked in the warm glow of the setting sun, Lara stumbled upon a crucial discovery in an obscure passage of an ancient manuscript. Alongside the cryptic message was a verse from Ecclesiastes 3:1, "To everything there is a season, and a time to every purpose under the heaven."

As the mysterious puzzle of the clock unraveled, a sense of foreboding descended upon Lara. With newfound determination, she resolved to uncover the true nature and purpose of the enigmatic timepiece, bracing herself for the secrets it held within its intricate mechanisms.

The clock did indeed control time, but it came at a terrible cost. Each tick of its hands drained the life force of those around it. Lara realized she had to hasten. She couldn't let the clock fall into the wrong hands, nor could she allow her father's work to bring harm to anyone. Under the cover of night, Lara made her way to Lord Randall's mansion, a foreboding structure that loomed on the outskirts of the village. She sneaked into his study, where the clock stood in all its dark glory. With trembling hands, she dismantled it, piece by piece, undoing the intricate work her father had poured his soul into.

In the dim light of the study, the ticking of the clock seemed to grow louder, almost mocking Lara's efforts. As she carefully removed each gear and cog, a sense of urgency gripped her heart. She knew that time was running out, both for those affected by the clock's malevolent power and for herself. Her actions weighed heavily on her, but she pushed forward, determined to right the wrongs set in motion.

With a final wrench, the clock fell silent. Lara stood there, panting, her hands stained with oil and sweat. The once imposing timepiece now lay in pieces before her, its dark magic broken. The sense of relief was palpable, but she knew her task was far from over. As she gathered the remnants of the clock, a new resolve filled her. She would undo the damage that had been done, to ensure that her father's legacy would not be one of destruction. With a heavy heart but a determined spirit, Lara left the mansion behind, carrying with her the remnants of the clock and a newfound sense of purpose.

But before she could finish, Lord Randall appeared, his eyes burning with fury. "You foolish girl! Do you know what you've done?" he roared. Lara's heart raced as she faced the wrath of the man who had wielded the clock's dark powers for so long. She steeled herself, ready to confront the consequences of her actions. Lord Randall's anger was like a storm, threatening to engulf her, but Lara stood her ground, determined to set things right.

As the confrontation unfolded, secrets long buried surfaced, revealing a history of manipulation and deceit. Lara realized the clock was not just a tool of power, but a symbol of the corruption that had plagued her family for generations. With each revelation, her resolve grew stronger, fueled by a sense of justice and a desire to break free from the shadows of the past.

In that moment, Lara understood her journey was not just about fixing a broken clock, but about reclaiming her family's honor and forging a new path forward. With Lord Randall's accusations ringing in her ears, she knew that the road ahead would be fraught with challenges and dangers. The broken clock in her hands offered a glimmer of hope. She could rewrite her troubled past.

Lara stood her ground, remembering another verse from Psalm 91:2: "I will say of the Lord, He is my refuge and my fortress: my God; in him will I trust." She declared with unwavering resolve, "I won't let you use this clock to harm anyone."

Faced with danger, Lara discovered a powerful incantation that banished Lord Randall, a malevolent figure, to the depths of time. With the clock's hands spinning wildly and a blinding light filling the room, Lara eliminated the threat, leaving her standing alone amidst the remnants of the dismantled clock. She carefully gathered the pieces and returned to her father's workshop, where she secured them away to prevent their misuse.

The town of Ellenwood prospered, thanks to the fortune left behind by Lord Randall. Lara, following in her father's footsteps, dedicated herself to crafting exquisite clocks that brought happiness to the villagers. Lara kept that night's remarkable events a secret. The tale of the Timekeeper's Daughter would serve as a testament to her bravery, unwavering belief, and the enduring power of time.

17

What Would You Do?

MARK 7:24-30

In the coastal town of Erie, where the waves whispered secrets and the sea breeze carried tales from distant lands, lived a woman named Esther. Esther was a devoted mother, and her life revolved around her daughter, Leah. A mysterious ailment afflicted Leah, a bright and joyful child, leaving her in constant distress. Desperate for a cure, Esther had tirelessly sought the aid of every healer and physician in the region, but to no avail.

One day, amidst the whispers of the townsfolk, Esther caught wind of a renowned teacher and healer named Jesus who had come to the region. With a newfound glimmer of hope in her heart, Esther made a solemn vow to seek Jesus and beseech him for help regardless of the challenges that lay ahead. Hopeful yet determined, Esther set out on a journey that would test her faith and resilience, all in the name of finding a cure for her beloved daughter Leah.

Jesus had entered a humble house on the outskirts of the town, seeking solace and rest from the demands of his ministry. He had hoped for a moment of peace, away from the crowds that constantly sought his attention. However, word of his presence spread quickly, and soon, Esther, a mother driven by the love for her daughter, found her way to the house. A mixture of hope and fear filled her heart as she approached Jesus, surrounded by his disciples.

Upon entering, Esther's eyes fell upon Jesus, the healer and teacher she had heard so much about. Overwhelmed by desperation, she fell to her knees before him and pleaded, "Lord, an unclean spirit possesses my daughter. Please, have mercy on her and heal her." Jesus, known for his compassion and miracles, gazed at her with a look that was both searching and wise.

In a moment that challenged Esther's faith, Jesus responded unexpectedly to her plea for healing for her daughter. Using a metaphor, he said, "Feed the children first; it's wrong to take the children's bread and throw it to the dogs." Despite her heart sinking, Esther's determination remained steadfast. With humility and unwavering faith, she replied, "Yes, Lord, but even the dogs under the table eat the children's crumbs." This exchange serves as a powerful example of Esther's resilience and belief in Jesus' ability to bring about healing.

Moved by her faith and persistence, Jesus smiled and said, "For this statement, you may go your way; the demon has left your daughter."

Esther's eyes welled with tears of gratitude as she hurried home, her heart filled with hope. As she entered her house in the quaint town of Erie, she saw Leah, her daughter, standing before her, free from the torment that had plagued her for so long. Mother and daughter embraced, their tears mingling as they rejoiced in their newfound peace.

The news of Leah's miraculous healing spread like wildfire throughout Erie, captivating the townspeople. They marveled at the power of faith and perseverance, witnessing firsthand the profound impact it can have. Esther's unwavering belief and determination had brought about a miracle, touching the lives of all who heard her story.

Esther's journey from despair to triumph became a beacon of hope for others in Erie. Her story served as a reminder that even in the darkest of times, holding onto faith and never giving up can lead to extraordinary outcomes. The townspeople found inspiration and solace in Esther and Leah's tale, reaffirming their own beliefs in the power of the human spirit.

As the sun set over Erie, a sense of unity and gratitude filled the air. Esther and Leah's bond, forged through trials and triumphs, stood as a testament to the resilience of the human heart. And in the hearts of the townspeople, a newfound sense of hope and possibility blossomed, fueled by the enduring power of faith and perseverance.

What would you have done with so much at stake? Faith is a powerful healer, and it was the faith of Esther that brought her daughter much-needed healing. How far would you go to save your friend, family member, or others? Jesus went all the way to Calvary's cross and shed His innocent blood there for everyone who would believe in His name.

In times of adversity and despair, faith can bring about miraculous healing and deliverance. Esther, a woman of unwavering faith, experienced the power of belief when her daughter needed healing. Through her faith, Esther could witness a profound miracle that changed the course of her daughter's life.

The question of how far one would go to save a loved one is profound. Would you be willing to make the ultimate sacrifice, as Jesus did on the cross, to ensure the well-being of those you hold dear? Jesus's selfless act of sacrificing his life for the salvation of humanity serves as a powerful example of unconditional love and unwavering faith.

In conclusion, the stories of Esther and Jesus exemplify the profound impact of faith and sacrifice. They remind us of the transformative power of belief and the lengths to which one can go to save others. Just as Esther's faith brought healing to her daughter and Jesus's sacrifice brought salvation to the world, may we also find the strength to stand firm in our faith and sacrifice for the well-being of those we cherish.

18

The Rebuke of His Disciples

LUKE 18:15

In the bustling town of Nazareth, where merchants haggled over goods and children played in the streets, an outstanding teacher named Jesus was passing through. Word of his miracles and teachings had spread everywhere, and people flocked to see him, hoping to catch a glimpse or hear his words. Among the crowd was a group of mothers, each holding their young children. Their eyes sparkled with hope as they approached Jesus, seeking his blessing for their little ones. As they drew near, the disciples, seeing the commotion, stepped forward to intervene. "Keep the children away," they said sternly. "The Master is busy, and you must not disturb him."

The scene captures a moment of tension and compassion as the mothers persist in their quest for Jesus' blessing, despite the disciples' attempts to deter them. This encounter sheds light on the inclusive nature of Jesus' teachings and the importance of embracing all individuals, regardless of age or status. Through this interaction, a powerful message of love and acceptance resonates, highlighting the transformative impact of a simple act of kindness.

The mothers, crestfallen and defeated, retreated as their hopes dashed. But in that moment, Jesus, perceiving the situation, called out to his disciples. His voice, though gentle, carried an underlying tone of rebuke as he spoke with authority. "Let the little children come to me, and do not hinder them," he declared. "For the kingdom of God belongs to such as these. Truly, I tell you, anyone who will not receive the kingdom of God like a little child will never enter it."

Upon hearing these words, the disciples were humbled and moved to step aside, allowing the mothers and their children to approach. Jesus kneeled, his eyes brimming with kindness, and extended his hands to bless each child individually. The children, in response, giggled and beamed with joy, their innocence and happiness gleaming like a warm ray of sunshine.

As the crowd watched in awe, they witnessed a profound lesson unfolding before their eyes. Surrounded by mothers and children, Jesus emphasized that the kingdom of God belonged not to the powerful or the learned but to those approaching with the pure, unpretentious faith of a child.

The mothers departed with hearts brimming with gratitude, and the children carried with them a cherished memory that would endure a lifetime. The disciples, too, gleaned a vital insight that day—one of humility, love, and the authentic essence of the kingdom of God. This poignant moment served as a reminder to all present of the importance of approaching life with a humble and loving heart.

In these passages and the story above, we can see the themes of love, betrayal, and redemption. Complex relationships mark the protagonist's journey, with love driving some characters to acts of betrayal, while others seek redemption for past wrongdoings. The interplay of these themes creates a rich tapestry of emotions and motivations that drive the narrative forward. Through the characters' choices and actions, we witness the power of love to both heal and harm and the possibility of redemption even in the face of betrayal.

We live in a complex world, where several factors such as technology, politics, economics, and social issues interplay to shape our daily lives. The rapid advancements in technology have interconnected the world like never, allowing for instant communication and access to information on a global scale. Political landscapes are constantly changing, affecting policies and relationships between nations. Intricate links between economic systems create a global market with far-reaching impacts. Social issues, such as inequality, climate change, and health crises, present ongoing challenges that require collective solutions. In this ever-evolving environment, navigating the complexities of our world requires adaptability, critical thinking, and a deep understanding of the interconnectedness of different systems.

Things were completely different in Jesus' day. A vastly different social, cultural, and political landscape characterized Jesus' time than ours today. In the first century AD, the region of the Roman Empire where Jesus lived was a melting pot of diverse religious beliefs, traditions, and practices. The Jewish people were under Roman rule, which significantly impacted their daily lives and interactions. The unique historical context of that era shaped the teachings of Jesus and the events that unfolded during his time.

In the situation described, Jesus responded in a manner that may seem unconventional by today's standards. His teachings of love, compassion, and forgiveness guided his actions and words. Jesus often emphasized understanding, empathy, and grace in his interactions with others, even in the face of adversity. This approach, rooted in his belief in the inherent dignity and worth of every individual, set him apart as a compassionate and wise leader. Jesus' response serves as a powerful example of how one can navigate challenging situations with humility, kindness, and a focus on reconciliation.

How the disciples of Jesus reacted to various situations and challenges has raised concerns among many. Their responses, as documented in the Bible, have been the subject of analysis and discussion among scholars and believers alike. Let's delve into some of the key instances where the disciples' reactions have sparked concern and contemplation.

1. **Lack of Understanding:**

One recurring theme in the Gospels is the disciples' failure to fully grasp the teachings and actions of Jesus. Despite being near their teacher, they often misunderstood his messages and intentions. This lack of comprehension led to confusion and misinterpretation of important spiritual truths.

2. **Fear and Doubt:**

Another common response of the disciples was fear and doubt, especially in times of crisis or uncertainty. When faced with challenges or threats, they would often react with fear and hesitation, questioning their own abilities and faith. Others viewed this response as weakness and a lack of trust in Jesus' power.

3. **Selfish Ambitions:**

The disciples displayed selfish ambitions and desires, seeking personal gain or recognition instead of focusing on the mission and teachings of Jesus. This self-centered attitude led to conflicts and tensions within the group, highlighting the importance of humility and selflessness in following Jesus.

The concerns raised by the responses of Jesus' disciples serve as a reminder of the complexities and struggles inherent in the journey of faith. By examining these reactions, we can learn valuable lessons about understanding, faith, and selflessness in following Jesus and living out his teachings.

19

Beware of the Scribes

LUKE 20:45-47

In the heart of Jerusalem, the Temple courts were bustling with activity. Merchants traded their goods, pilgrims offered their sacrifices, and the religious leaders, known as scribes, moved about with an air of authority. Among the crowd, a humble fisher named Benjamin stood quietly, observing the scene. Benjamin had heard whispers of an outstanding teacher named Jesus, who spoke with wisdom and authority. As he watched, Jesus stepped forward and instructed the people. His voice was calm but carried the weight of truth.

In the bustling city of Jerusalem, amidst a crowd gathered in the Temple courtyard, Benjamin found himself captivated by the teachings of Jesus. As the sun set, casting a warm glow over the scene, Benjamin felt a profound connection to the words that Jesus spoke. The surrounding crowd hung on every word, and Benjamin marveled at the way Jesus effortlessly reached out to people from all levels of society.

Jesus's teachings provided Benjamin with comfort and clarity, sparking a sense of curiosity and faith within his soul. This encounter marked a pivotal moment in Benjamin's life, igniting a journey of spiritual discovery that would take him to unexpected places. Amid the noise and chaos of the crowded courtyard, Benjamin found a sense of peace and purpose that he had never experienced before. The profound impact of that day's encounter stayed with Benjamin forever, shaping his beliefs and guiding him on a path of understanding and hope. Benjamin pondered Jesus' words and the deep connection he felt. The man's wisdom and grace had profoundly and permanently altered his life.

Benjamin's encounter with Jesus was a transformative experience that left an indelible mark on his soul.

The teachings of Jesus provided him with a newfound sense of comfort and clarity, igniting a curiosity and faith that would shape his spiritual journey in profound ways. Amidst the hustle and bustle of the crowded courtyard, Benjamin found a moment of tranquility and purpose that resonated deeply within him. The words of Jesus, spoken with authority and grace, had a lasting impact on Benjamin, guiding him towards a path of understanding and hope.

In a pivotal moment in Benjamin's life, he experienced a transformative encounter with Jesus that became a catalyst for his spiritual growth. This encounter led Benjamin to explore new avenues of faith and belief, shaping his worldview in profound ways. The wisdom and compassion exhibited by Jesus made a lasting impact on Benjamin, leaving him with a sense of connection and purpose that he carried forward on his journey. Reflecting on the encounter, Benjamin remained forever grateful for the teachings of Jesus and the transformative power they held. Jesus's words warning about the scribes, who seek recognition and wealth at the expense of others, resonated deeply with Benjamin, solidifying his commitment to a path of humility and service.

The words struck a chord with Benjamin. He had always admired the scribes for their knowledge and piety, but he had also witnessed their hypocrisy. He recalled the times when they had exploited the vulnerable, taking advantage of their position to enrich themselves. As Jesus continued to teach, a widow approached the Temple Treasury. She dropped in two small copper coins, which was all she had to live on. The clink of the coins was barely audible, but Jesus noticed.

Turning to his disciples, he said, "Truly, I tell you, this poor widow has put in more than all the others."

In this poignant moment, Benjamin grasped a profound truth about devotion and sacrifice. He understood that the widow's simple act of giving, despite her own lack, spoke volumes about her faith and commitment to God. It was a stark contrast to the ostentatious displays of wealth and power he had seen from the scribes. Through Jesus' words, Benjamin learned that true spirituality transcends material wealth and societal status. It is the sincerity of one's intentions and the depth of one's connection to God that truly matter. The widow's offering became a symbol of selflessness and trust, inspiring Benjamin to reevaluate his own values and beliefs.

From that day forward, Benjamin's perspective shifted. He no longer admired the scribes for their outward displays of piety but sought to emulate the widow's genuine faith and humility. He dedicated himself to living a life of integrity, helping those in need, and seeking the truth in Jesus' teachings. As the days passed, the people of Jerusalem saw through the facade of the scribes. They recognized the wisdom in Jesus' words and the importance of humility and genuine faith. The message of "Beware of the Scribes" resonated throughout the city, transforming hearts and minds.

The story of Benjamin's transformation serves as a powerful reminder of the true essence of faith and humility. It illustrates the impact of genuine actions over mere appearances and how a sincere dedication to living with integrity can inspire others to do the same. The shift in perspective among the people of Jerusalem highlights the transformative power of authentic faith and the recognition of true wisdom. Through Benjamin's example, the city experienced a profound change, with the message of humility and genuine faith spreading everywhere.

As the community embraced these values, a new sense of unity and purpose emerged. People prioritized helping those in need and seeking the truth in Jesus' teachings rather than following the empty displays of piety exhibited by the scribes. Benjamin's transformation inspired individuals throughout the city to live with integrity and authenticity. The lesson learned from this experience was clear: true faith and humility have the power to transform hearts and minds, leading to a more compassionate and enlightened society.

20

The Scholar of Alexandria

LUKE 21:17-19

In the ancient city of Alexandria, known for its grand library and bustling marketplaces, lived a young scholar named Rebekah. Rebekah had a fervent desire for knowledge and spent her days immersed in scrolls, seeking wisdom and understanding. The city was a melting pot of cultures and ideas, drawing scholars and traders from everywhere.

Despite its vibrancy, Alexandria was also a place of turmoil and strife. Political tensions and religious conflicts often disrupted the peace, and the people lived in constant fear of persecution. Amidst this chaotic backdrop, Rebekah's thirst for knowledge only grew stronger, driving her to delve deeper into the mysteries of the world.

As she navigated the complexities of life in Alexandria, she found solace in the pages of ancient texts and the company of fellow scholars who shared her passion for learning. Rebekah's journey in this city of wonders and dangers would test her resolve and shape her understanding of the world in profound ways.

Rebekah, a devout follower of the teachings of Jesus, faced numerous challenges on her spiritual journey. Daily challenges tested her unwavering faith as she encountered opposition from those who did not share her beliefs. Despite these obstacles, Rebekah remained resolute, drawing strength from the words of her beloved teacher.

One memorable evening, Rebekah gathered with fellow believers in a secret chamber to seek solace and guidance. Together, they found comfort in reading from the teachings of Jesus, which included a profound message about enduring persecution for the sake of their faith.

This passage reminded Rebekah and her companions that their struggles were not in vain and that their ultimate reward awaited them in the afterlife. These moments reinforced Rebekah's commitment to her faith, inspiring her to stand firm against adversity and continue her path with unwavering determination.

Amid escalating persecution in Alexandria, Rebekah found solace in the words that echoed in her heart. She understood the gravity of the danger that loomed over her path, yet she embraced the virtues of patience and perseverance with unwavering determination. Each passing day brought more menacing threats, compelling Rebekah and her fellow believers to seek refuge in the shadows and constantly evade detection.

Their faith became their guiding light, the anchor that steadied them amidst the turbulent storm of uncertainty. One night, Rebekah sat alone, struggling with their troubles. Jesus' words echoed in her mind: "In patience, possess your soul."

Through the trials and tribulations that tested their faith, Rebekah's unwavering commitment and steadfastness gleamed, illustrating the power of faith in the face of adversity. With renewed determination, Rebekah became a source of encouragement for her fellow believers. She reminded them of the importance of patience and the promise of eternal life. Together, they faced their trials with unwavering faith, finding solace in knowing that their souls were secure in God's hands.

In a world filled with uncertainties and challenges, Rebekah's story serves as a beacon of hope and inspiration. Her resilience in the face of adversity highlights the transformative power of faith. By standing firm in her beliefs and offering unwavering support to her community, Rebekah exemplifies the strength that comes from trusting in God's plan.

As Rebekah navigated the difficulties of life, she held onto her faith as an anchor, guiding her through the darkest of times. Her unwavering commitment to God's teachings not only sustained her but also uplifted those around her. Through her actions and words, Rebekah instilled a sense of hope and perseverance in her fellow believers, reminding them that no trial is too great when faced with faith.

In conclusion, Rebekah's journey is a testament to the power of faith in overcoming adversity. Her story serves as a reminder that through unwavering commitment and trust in God, one can find strength and solace even in the most challenging of circumstances. Rebekah's legacy lives on as a beacon of light, inspiring others to hold fast to their faith and trust in the promise of eternal life.

As the years passed, the city of Alexandria transformed from its architecture to its cultural landscape. However, amidst these changes, the legacy of Rebekah remained a steadfast presence. Her remarkable story of patience and perseverance continued to inspire and resonate with the residents of Alexandria, serving as a guiding light for future generations.

Rebekah's unwavering faith in the face of adversity stood as a testament to the resilience of the human spirit and the enduring power of belief. Through her example, she left behind a legacy that transcended time, offering hope and encouragement to all who faced challenges in their lives. Rebekah's story became woven into the fabric of the city, a reminder of the strength that lies within everyone to overcome obstacles and emerge stronger on the other side.

The human spirit is a remarkable entity, possessing a vast array of capabilities and potential. From acts of courage and resilience to feats of creativity and compassion, the human spirit is a driving force behind many remarkable achievements throughout history. It is this intangible essence within everyone that propels us to over-come challenges, pursue our dreams, and connect with others on a profound level. The human spirit is a source of inspiration and motivation, constantly pushing us to strive for greatness and make a positive impact on the world.

21

A New Creature

———— ❈ ————

II CORINTHIANS 5:17-19

I n the bustling city of Corinth, where commerce
thrived and cultures mingled, lived a man named
Samuel. People knew Samuel for his shrewd business acumen, but greed and deceit characterized his life. He had
amassed wealth through dubious means, leaving a trail of
broken relationships and betrayed trust in his wake.

One day, while wandering through the marketplace,
Samuel heard a group of people discussing the teachings
of a man named Paul. Intrigued by their passionate conversation, he lingered nearby, listening to Paul's words:

"Therefore, if anyone is in Christ, he is a new creation; the old has passed away, behold, the new has come. All this is from God, who through Christ reconciled us to himself and gave us the ministry of reconciliation; in Christ, God was reconciling the world to himself, not counting their trespasses against them, and entrusting to us the message of reconciliation."

As Samuel absorbed these words, a stirring of conviction and hope took root in his heart. Could it be possible for someone like him, tainted by his past misdeeds, to experience a new beginning through Christ's message of reconciliation? The bustling city of Corinth held within it the promise of redemption for Samuel, a man grappling with the consequences of his actions and seeking a path to transformation.

The words struck a chord deep within Samuel, a wealthy man who felt empty and burdened by his past actions. Despite his material accomplishments, a sense of dissatisfaction lingered within him. However, the idea of leaving his old ways behind and becoming a new creature resonated with Samuel. This newfound perspective sparked a glimmer of hope within him, prompting him to seek Paul and take part in his gatherings.

As Samuel immersed himself in Paul's teachings, he grasped the transformative power of Christ's love and forgiveness. Over time, his heart softened, and he felt a profound desire to change his ways. Through his interactions with Paul and the understanding gained from the teachings, Samuel embarked on a journey of self-discovery and spiritual growth. This marked the beginning of a significant transformation in Samuel's life as he embraced the principles of love, forgiveness, and renewal.

One evening, after a moving sermon, Samuel approached Paul and confessed his past misdeeds. With tears in his eyes, he asked for guidance on how to make amends and become a new creature in Christ. Paul compassionately put a hand on Samuel's shoulder. "Seek forgiveness from God and those you've hurt," he advised. "It won't be easy, but with faith and determination, you can reconcile with those you have hurt and start anew."

With Paul's words as his guiding light, Samul embarked on a journey of reconciliation. He visited those he had wronged, offering sincere apologies, and making restitution wherever possible. Some forgave him, while others were not as quick to forget, but Samuel persisted, fueled by his newfound faith.

Each encounter was a step towards redemption, and Samuel found solace in taking responsibility for his actions and seeking forgiveness. Through this process, he not only sought to mend broken relationships but also to heal his own spirit and find peace in the forgiveness of others.

As Samuel continued his path of reconciliation, he learned valuable lessons about humility, forgiveness, and the transformative power of faith. His journey was not without challenges, but with each apology offered and each restitution made, he felt a weight lifted off his shoulders. Samuel's story showed that forgiveness is possible, even for the worst of sins. Genuine change comes from repentance and a commitment to love and compassion.

As time passed, Samuel's transformation became clear. His once hardened heart was now filled with compassion and generosity. He used his business acumen to help others, providing opportunities for those in need and supporting charitable causes. The people of Corinth saw Samuel in a new light, not as the greedy businessperson he once was but as a living testament to the power of redemption and transformation. Samuel's story inspired others to seek their own paths of reconciliation and renewal, spreading the message of hope and forgiveness throughout the city.

Samuel's journey serves as a powerful example of how individuals can change for the better and make a positive impact on their communities. His commitment to giving back and supporting those less fortunate highlights the profound effect that personal growth and transformation can have on society. Through his actions, Samuel has become a beacon of hope and a source of inspiration for all who encounter his story.

In Christianity, the concept of becoming a new creature in Christ is a central belief that emphasizes the transformative power of faith. The Bible's teachings, especially 2 Corinthians 5:17, root this idea: "Therefore, if anyone is in Christ, the new creation has come: The old has gone, the new is here!"

The process of becoming a new creature in Christ involves letting go of one's old sinful nature and being renewed in the image of Christ. It signifies a complete transformation of the heart, mind, and spirit, leading to a life guided by the principles of love, grace, and righteousness. This concept serves as a foundational truth for many

Christians, inspiring them to live a life dedicated to serving God and following the teachings of Jesus.

The themes of transformation, reconciliation, and becoming a new creature in Christ symbolize the profound changes that individuals can undergo through their faith and spiritual journey.

Transformation signifies the process of inner growth and renewal, where individuals develop into their best selves. Reconciliation represents the healing of broken relationships, both with oneself and with others, through forgiveness and acceptance. Becoming a new creature in Christ reflects the idea of rebirth and starting anew in alignment with Christian values and beliefs. These themes are powerful symbols of personal growth, redemption, and the transformative power of faith.

The Christian faith is a transformative journey that begins with a new birth, symbolizing a spiritual rebirth and a fresh start in the eyes of God. This new birth brings a renewed mind, a process of spiritual growth and enlightenment leading to a deeper understanding of God's love and purpose for our lives.

Christian faith centers on forsaking past sins, admitting flaws, and seeking forgiveness through repentance. This involves committing to live according to God's will. Christians believe in Christ's sacrifice on the cross for humanity's redemption. They trust in Him as their redeemer and follow His teachings to live a life of faith, love, and service.

Through this journey of transformation, Christians strive to embody the values of compassion, forgiveness, and humility, reflecting the grace and mercy of God in their interactions with others.

May God continue to bless you on your journey today.

22

Delight in the Lord

PROVERBS 15:6-9

I n the serene village of Gildan, nestled amidst rolling hills and meandering streams, lived a wise and kind-hearted man named Daniel. The villagers held Daniel in high esteem for his unwavering integrity and deep faith in God. His humble abode served as a beacon of tranquility and abundance, where love and compassion flowed freely. Daniel's presence in Gildan was not just a blessing to the villagers but a source of inspiration and guidance for all who crossed his path. His wisdom and generosity knew no bounds, making him a revered figure in the community.

Through his actions and teachings, Daniel embodied the virtues of goodness and selflessness, leaving an indelible mark on the hearts of those around him.

One day, a traveler named Caleb arrived in Gildan. Caleb was a wealthy merchant, but he had amassed his riches through dishonest means. Guilt burdened his heart, and he sought true peace and contentment. As Caleb walked through the village, he heard the locals speak highly of Daniel and his righteous ways. Intrigued, Caleb sought Daniel's counsel. He approached Daniel's home and found him tending to his garden. "Greetings, Daniel," Caleb began. "Your wisdom and devotion to the Lord are renowned. My troubled heart has led me to seek your guidance."

Caleb's journey to Gildan was not just a physical one but also a spiritual quest for redemption. His encounter with Daniel, a man known for his integrity and connection to the divine, marked a turning point in Caleb's life. The lush surroundings of Gildan provided a fitting backdrop for this transformative moment, as nature often mirrors the inner workings of the soul. The meeting between Caleb and Daniel held the promise of wisdom, forgiveness, and a path towards true peace for the troubled traveler.

Daniel looked up from his work and invited Caleb to sit with him. "Tell me, my friend, what weighs upon your heart?" Caleb sighed and confessed, "I have amassed great wealth, but my methods have been less than honorable. I have deceived and taken advantage of others to achieve my success. Despite my riches, I find no peace or joy in my heart."

Daniel listened intently and then recited a passage from the Proverbs: "The house of the righteous contains great treasure, but the income of the wicked brings ruin. The lips of the wise spread knowledge, but the hearts of fools are not upright. Prayers from the upright please the Lord, although he despises sacrifices from the wicked. The Lord detests the way of the wicked, but he loves those who pursue righteousness."

Caleb pondered these words, feeling the weight of his actions pressing on his conscience. The wisdom shared by Daniel stirred a sense of reflection and contemplation within him. Would he continue down the path of deceit and greed, or would he seek to amend his ways and find true fulfillment in righteousness? The choice lay before him, challenging him to confront his inner turmoil and make a decision that would shape his future.

Daniel's words inspired Caleb, teaching him that true wealth lies in a righteous and honest heart, not material possessions. Inspired by this wisdom, Caleb asked Daniel for guidance on how to make amends and find genuine delight in the Lord. Daniel advised Caleb to seek forgiveness from those he had wronged, restore unjustly taken possessions, and dedicate his life to pursuing righteousness. He emphasized the importance of turning away from deceit and dishonesty and living with integrity and kindness, as these are traits that bring delight to the Lord.

With Daniel's gentle guidance, Caleb embarked on a journey of repentance and transformation. He reached out to those he had wronged, offering sincere apologies, and making restitution. By changing his ways and embracing a life of integrity, Caleb discovered a newfound sense of peace and joy that had eluded him in the past. This story serves as a powerful reminder of the transformative power of seeking forgiveness, living with integrity, and walking in the ways of the Lord.

The residents of Gildan bore witness to Caleb's remarkable transformation, which left them deeply inspired. The

profound impact of righteousness and the authentic joy
that radiated from living a life under the teachings of the
Lord astounded them. Caleb's journey served as a beacon
of hope and a testament to the transformative power of
faith and devotion. His story resonated with the community, illuminating the path towards spiritual fulfillment
and true happiness. Caleb's experience in Gildan stands as
a testament to the enduring influence of living a virtuous
and purposeful life.

The themes of righteousness, repentance, and the genuine delight that come from living a life pleasing to the
Lord are prevalent throughout various scriptures. These
themes serve as guiding principles for believers, emphasizing the importance of living a virtuous and faithful life.

Righteousness is a central theme in scripture, highlighting the significance of moral uprightness and adherence to
divine laws. The concept of righteousness is often associated with the justice, integrity, and purity of the heart. God
portrays righteousness as a key characteristic of those who
obey his commandments.

Repentance is another prominent theme in scripture,
emphasizing the act of turning away from sin and return-
ing to God. Through repentance, individuals acknowl-

edge their wrongdoing, seek forgiveness, and strive to live under God's will. It is a transformative process that leads to spiritual growth and renewal.

The genuine delight that comes from living a life pleasing to the Lord is a recurring motif in scripture. The joy and fulfillment believers experience when aligning their actions and attitudes with God's purposes root this delight. This life, pleasing to the Lord, is a source of inner peace, contentment, and spiritual abundance that transcend earthly pleasures.

In conclusion, the themes of righteousness, repentance, and the genuine delight found in scripture serve as foundational principles for believers seeking to deepen their relationship with God. Embracing these themes encourages individuals to strive for moral excellence, seek reconciliation with God, and find ultimate satisfaction in a life that honors and glorifies the Lord.

May the Lord richly bless you on your journey today!

23

The All-in-One Pill

PHILIPPIANS 4:4

I magine a world where a single pill could address all our physical, mental, and spiritual needs. The concept of a miraculous pill that can solve every insignificant problem we face is undoubtedly appealing. If such a pill existed, it would undoubtedly attract a significant following, with people eagerly seeking it out as a solution to their multifaceted challenges.

The idea of a one-size-fits-all pill has long been a subject of fascination and speculation. The allure of a remedy that could provide relief for physical ailments, mental health issues, and spiritual well-being is undeniable. In a fast-paced world where individuals are constantly seeking solutions to enhance their quality of life, the concept of a universal pill that offers comprehensive benefits is particularly enticing.

From alleviating physical pain to enhancing cognitive function and promoting inner peace, the potential applications of such a pill are vast. The convenience and efficiency of addressing multiple dimensions of wellness with a single dose make the idea even more appealing. The prospect of a pill that could bring about holistic healing and balance is an interesting vision that resonates with many.

A pastor friend once told me a funny story about a recently married elderly couple. The tale goes that Margaret and John, the newlyweds, were enjoying a quiet moment at the kitchen table when Margaret nonchalantly took out a bottle of pills and swallowed one. Concerned, John inquired about the medication, to which Margaret clarified the pills were a blend of vitamins and herbs aimed at rejuvenating her. Intrigued, John requested to try one himself.

The following day, Margaret couldn't find John inside the house, which puzzled her. Upon stepping outside, she discovered him sitting on the curb, visibly upset. Sensing his distress, Margaret inquired about the reason for his tears, only to be met with an unexpected revelation: John was distraught because he had missed the school bus!

This humorous tale shows one is never too old to be youthful.

Human suffering is a universal experience that touches every individual. It encompasses a wide range of physical, emotional, and mental pain that numerous factors, such as illness, loss, trauma, or societal injustices can cause. While the degree and nature of suffering may vary from person to person, it is a common thread that binds humanity together. Despite our best efforts to avoid or ease suffering, it remains an inescapable part of the human condition. From personal struggles to global crises, the reality of human suffering serves as a reminder of our shared vulnerability and resilience.

While the concept that a miracle pill can solve all our problems remains a fantasy, the desire for a comprehensive solution to our diverse needs is a universal longing. The pursuit of well-being and fulfillment drives individuals to seek innovative approaches to enhance their lives. Although a magical pill may be out of reach, the quest for holistic wellness continues to inspire hope and exploration in the realm of health and self-improvement.

A holistic approach to wellness is a way of looking at health that considers the whole person—mind, body, and spirit. It emphasizes the connection between distinct aspects of a person's life and how they can affect overall well-being. This approach focuses on addressing the underlying causes of health issues rather than just treating symptoms. It often includes a combination of lifestyle factors, such as nutrition, exercise, stress management, and mental health practices. Holistic wellness also considers social, emotional, and environmental factors that can affect health. By focusing on the whole person and all aspects of their life, an integrated approach aims to promote overall well-being and prevent illness.

As Christians, we must constantly remind ourselves that we are people of joy. This means that even in the face of challenges and difficulties, we are called to maintain a spirit of joy and hope. Our faith teaches us that joy is not dependent on our circumstances but is a gift from God that can sustain us through all trials. By embracing our identity as people of joy, we can spread love, peace, and positivity to those around us, reflecting the light of Christ in our lives. Let us strive to cultivate a deep sense of joy in our hearts, knowing that it is a powerful witness to the transformative power of the gospel.

When we consider the word "Gospel," we recall its meaning: good news. The term "Gospel" originates from the Old English word "godspel," which is a translation of the Greek word "euangelion," meaning good news or glad tidings. In a religious context, the Gospel refers to the teachings and message of Jesus Christ as recorded in the New Testament of the Bible. Christians consider it the core message of their faith, emphasizing salvation and redemption through faith in Jesus. The Gospel is often associated with hope, love, and the promise of eternal life, making it a central theme in Christian theology and practice. Through the Gospel, believers find comfort, guidance, and inspiration to live a life of faith and service.

Amid the ever-changing and tumultuous world we live in, the Word of God stands as an immovable pillar of strength and guidance. Despite the swirling winds of doubt, anger, frustration, and pain that may buffet us, God's Word remains steadfast, unchanging, and constant. It serves as a source of comfort, wisdom, and stability during life's storms, offering hope and assurance in times of uncertainty.

Like a steadfast lighthouse, God's Word shines, guiding us through darkness toward truth and righteousness. Let us take refuge in the unchanging and eternal Word of God, for in it we find solace, peace, and unwavering truth.

The apostle Paul is a fitting example of perseverance and faith in the face of adversity. Despite enduring multiple trials, tribulations, and even being stoned and imprisoned, he never wavered in his commitment to his beliefs. Despite being mocked and ridiculed for his faith, Paul remained steadfast and wrote inspiring words to his churches, encouraging them to "Rejoice in the Lord always." His unwavering spirit and resilience in the face of challenges serve as a powerful example for believers throughout history. It is a testament to his deep faith and conviction that he could find joy and peace even amid suffering and persecution.

As Christians, we are called to be beacons of hope and joy in a world that often feels dark and challenging. We face many trials. Faith in the Lord sustains us through them. Let us hold fast to the teachings of Jesus and continue to walk in His ways, spreading His message of love and compassion to all we encounter.

By embodying hope and joy in our daily lives, we can inspire others to seek the light of Christ and find solace in His eternal promises. Let us stand firm in our faith, trusting in the Lord's guidance and embracing the peace that surpasses all understanding.

24

Faith and Fear

JOHN 20:19

John 20:19 describes Jesus' appearance to His disciples after His resurrection:

That first day of the week, while the disciples were meeting behind locked doors, fearing the Jewish leaders, Jesus appeared among them, saying, "Peace be with you!" (John 20:19, NIV).

Fear and uncertainty gripped the disciples, who huddled behind locked doors, mourning the loss of their spiritual guide, whom the Romans had crucified. Left alone and in a state of despair, they yearned for reassurance. It was in this vulnerable moment that Jesus entered their midst, offering them peace and hope. His presence brought about a profound transformation, dispelling their fear, and instilling in them a sense of calm and assurance. The message of peace that emanated from Jesus' very being was not merely comforting but deeply profound, reminding them of the transcendent power of his presence.

Anxiety can be overwhelming in our lives. I remember once when I faced a major life decision. Fear was rampant in my life, and I searched everywhere for a solution. It was during a camp meeting sermon some days later that I heard a minister expound upon God's peace. Within me, I felt an overwhelming sense of calm and clarity emanating from his words. Even amid the chaos in our lives, God's peace can transform our hearts and minds.

In those early days of my ministry, I struggled with doubts about my faith. What minister hasn't? I was questioning everything, looking for answers, and felt spiritually lost. While reading John 20:19 one night, I realized Jesus appeared to His fearful and doubting disciples and brought them immense comfort. It reminded me, in that moment, that Jesus had come to me as well to meet me in my doubts and fears, offering His sweet peace and assurance.

Let me share with you some scripture that will hopefully enlighten your spirit.

1. **Philippians 4:6-7:**

"Do not be anxious about anything, but in every situation, by prayer and petition, with thanksgiving, present your requests to God. And the peace of God, which transcends all understanding, will guard your hearts and your minds in Christ Jesus."

This verse complements John 20:19 by emphasizing that God's peace is beyond human understanding and is available to us through prayer and thanksgiving.

2. **Isaiah 41:10**:

"So do not fear, for I am with you; do not be dismayed, for I am your God. I will strengthen you and help you; I will uphold you with my righteous right hand."

Just as Jesus reassured His disciples with His presence, this verse reminds us that God's presence is a source of strength and courage, eliminating fear and dismay.

In times of uncertainty and challenges, the promise of God's presence offers comfort and assurance. It serves as a reminder that we are not alone in our struggles, for He is always by our side, ready to strengthen and uphold us. This verse reflects the unwavering support and love that God provides to His children, instilling confidence and faith in the face of adversity. Just as Jesus stood with His disciples, God stands with us today, offering solace and empowerment to navigate life's trials.

3. **Psalm 34:4:**

"I sought the Lord, and he answered me; he delivered me from all my fears."

Seeking the Lord and experiencing His deliverance from fear aligns with the disciples' experience of Jesus' peace in John 20:19.

John 20:19 is a powerful reminder of the transformative peace that Jesus brings, especially in times of fear and uncertainty. In this verse, we see Jesus appearing to his disciples after his resurrection, despite the doors being locked in fear of the Jews. The peace that Jesus offers transcends physical barriers and brings a sense of calm to his followers. This message is deeply relevant today as we navigate personal crises, doubts, and anxiety.

Jesus' post-resurrection appearance (John 20:19) is a beacon of hope. His presence and peace are available, even when we're afraid or uncertain. The reassurance that we are never alone and that His peace is always within reach is a comforting truth that can anchor us in the storms of life. This verse and related scriptures offer solace and strength. The Prince of Peace is with us, calming our fears and bringing peace beyond understanding.

As we meditate on John 20:19, let us remember Jesus' enduring promise of peace. Let us hold on to this truth and find comfort in the presence of our Savior, who brings peace that the world cannot give.

A few years ago, a close friend of mine experienced the sudden loss of their parent, which plunged them into deep grief and emotional turmoil. Overwhelm consumed them, much like the fear and uncertainty that locked away the disciples. However, during this dark period, my friend turned to prayer and scripture for comfort. Specifically, John 20:19, where Jesus greets his disciples with "Peace be with you," became a beacon of hope for them. This verse served as a reminder that even amid profound loss, Jesus is present, offering peace and reassurance. Through this passage, my friend found the strength to navigate their grief, knowing that they were not alone and that the peace of Jesus was always within reach.

I once knew someone who was facing a major career change, and the uncertainty was daunting. They had just left a stable job to pursue a passion project, and the fear of failure was ever-present. During this time, they leaned heavily on their faith and the teachings of the Bible. The locked doors the disciples faced in John 20:19 symbolized the barriers and fears my friend was encountering. Yet Jesus' appearance and His message of peace provided a powerful reminder that they could find tranquility and assurance in their journey. This encouragement helped them push through the uncertainty and find success and fulfillment in their alternative career path.

Amid doubt and apprehension, my friend found solace in the words of the Bible, drawing strength from the story of the disciples' encounter with Jesus. Just as the disciples locked themselves in a room, feeling trapped and uncertain, my friend understood their struggles. However, the transformative moment when Jesus appeared, offering peace and reassurance, served as a turning point in their own journey.

My friend's faith and trust provided peace and confidence during their career transition. They navigated the challenges with newfound ease. Despite the obstacles and uncertainties that lay ahead, they found the courage to persevere, fueled by the belief that a higher purpose guided their path.

Through moments of reflection and prayer, my friend discovered the inner strength to overcome their fears and embrace the unknown. With each step forward, they found themselves closer to realizing their dreams and aspirations, empowered by the unwavering faith that had sustained them through the darkest moments of uncertainty.

In the end, my friend's story serves as a testament to the transformative power of faith in the face of uncertainty. By holding onto their beliefs and trusting in the journey laid out before them, they could find peace, assurance, and success in their alternative career path.

Epilogue

"Whispers on the Wind" was the title of my last published book. The title itself carries within it a sense of mystery and intrigue. This book delves into the enigmatic world of communication with nature's gentle whispers, exploring the unseen connections that bind us to the surrounding elements. Through poetic prose and vivid imagery, "Whispers on the Wind" invites readers to listen closely to the subtle messages carried on the breeze, inviting them to uncover the secrets hidden within the rustling leaves and swirling gusts of wind. With each page turned, the book draws the reader deeper into a world where whispers speak louder than words, where the wind carries messages of hope, love, and wisdom.

Just as there are "whispers" everywhere, I am reminded that the Holy Spirit, the third person of the trinity of the Father, Son, and Holy Spirit, is also everywhere. People often describe the Holy Spirit as God's divine presence within the world, guiding and comforting believers. This omnipresence of the Holy Spirit is a foundational belief in Christianity, emphasizing the constant connection between God and His people. Believers experience the Holy Spirit's presence in every aspect of their lives, providing strength, wisdom, and guidance during times of need. Through prayer, reflection, and faith, individuals can cultivate a deeper awareness of the Holy Spirit's presence and experience the transformative power of divine guidance.

The Holy Spirit is a central figure in Christian theology, often referred to as the third person of the Holy Trinity. Christians believe God sends the Holy Spirit, a divine being, to guide, empower, and comfort believers. The Holy Spirit is the source of spiritual gifts, such as wisdom, knowledge, faith, healing, and prophecy. The New Testament depicts the Holy Spirit's descent on Jesus at his baptism and its empowerment of the early disciples at Pentecost. Christians believe that the Holy Spirit continues to be active in the world today, working in the hearts and lives of believers to lead them in truth and righteousness.

Here are some references to the Holy Spirit in scripture:

1. The book of Acts describes the Holy Spirit descending upon the apostles on Pentecost, filling them with power and enabling them to speak in different languages.

2. In the Gospel of John, Jesus promises to send the Holy Spirit as a comforter and helper to his disciples after his departure.

3. Paul's letters frequently cite the Holy Spirit as the source of spiritual gifts and the one empowering believers to live a life pleasing to God.

4. The Bible portrays the Holy Spirit as the third person of the Trinity, equal in power and authority to God the Father and God the Son.

Tapestries of Life is a thought-provoking new book that offers a unique perspective on the Holy Spirit and its intricate relationships with God. Through a series of insightful reflections and interpretations, this book delves into the profound and complex nature of the Holy Spirit, shedding light on its role within the divine trinity. This book invites you to deepen your understanding of the spiritual realm by exploring the spiritual tapestries woven by the Holy Spirit and contemplating the dynamic interactions between the Holy Spirit and God.

As I reach its conclusion, I pray that these short stories and articles further enhance your journey through life. They should guide you and enable you to become the best you can. While it is bittersweet for me, as the writer to conclude this work, I am already full of the excitement and anticipation of the next. I will press forward towards the mark of God's higher calling with each new day and each new story. Thank you for sharing this with me.

The Rev. Dr. Charles E. Cravey

March 1, 2025

Afterword

As I close this chapter of my life and this book, I look around outside, and something is creeping forward. Spring is on its way. The daffodils and jonquils are in full bloom, their vibrant colors signaling the start of a new season. My Elm trees, flowering pear trees, and others are popping out all over the yard, their branches adorned with delicate blossoms that sway in the gentle breeze. Our blueberry bushes are leafing, their fresh green leaves unfurling as they prepare to bear fruit. The world is pregnant with fresh growth, each plant and tree bursting with life and vitality. Spring is a time of renewal and transformation, a reminder that even in the darkest of times, there is always the promise of new beginnings.

Unique weather events and challenges marked the past winter in the southern region. It began with the first snowfall in a decade, where four inches of snow blanketed the area. Despite the usual shutdown that occurs when snow hits the south, residents found joy in witnessing this rare occurrence. However, winter was further complicated by the aftermath of Hurricane Helene, which brought havoc and destruction to the region.

Following the memorable hurricane, Helene. She struck the area just before the official start of winter. The hurricane caused widespread damage, leaving residents grappling with the aftermath. The chaos caused by Helene made it difficult for people to access essential services, with many struggling to make trips to town because of blocked roads and limited resources.

One of the major challenges faced by the community was the scarcity of fuel. Long queues of people overwhelmed gas stations as they tried to buy gas for their generators and cars. The power outages caused by the hurricane left many residents relying on generators to keep their freezers running and prevent their food from spoiling. The high demand for gas led to shortages and extended waiting times, adding to the difficulties faced by the community.

The tough winter in the southern region, characterized by an unusual snowfall and the aftermath of Hurricane Helene, tested the resilience of the community. Despite the challenges, residents came together to overcome the obstacles and support each other during these trying times. Winter served as a reminder of the unpredictable nature of weather and the importance of preparedness in the face of natural disasters.

I've been incredibly busy, consumed by the demands of my writing projects, leaving little time for anything else. My wife is continually curious about the origin of my creative material, but divine inspiration flows freely to those who are receptive to it. I'm afraid I cannot offer any further explanation beyond what I have already provided.

In the past month, I have poured my heart and soul into creating seven unique pieces of literature that have been well-received by readers. This burst of creativity and productivity has been a testament to the power of faith and inspiration. With each book, I have delved deep into my spiritual connection, allowing divine guidance to shape my words and ideas.

As I continue this writing journey, I am grateful for the blessings and insights that come my way. Through dedication and a willingness to listen to the whispers of the divine, I have been able to channel my creativity into tangible works that resonate with others. Each book reflects the divine spark within me, a gift that I am humbled to share with the world.

Besides the current work in progress, there are four other books in the infantile stage that I am looking forward to completing before the summer is in full bloom. Setting ambitious goals for myself, I strive to write at least three articles or short stories every day. Stephen King inspired this daily writing routine; he advised aspiring writers to aim for at least 3,000 words per day. Despite the challenge, I am proud to say that I have successfully met this target. The problem is when to quit!

As spring arrives, I feel the age of my seventy-three years creeping up on me. Arthritis, four back surgeries, and other dilemmas have attempted to slow me down, but I've fought back with every fiber within, and, thus far, I've won. My eyesight, because of the extreme writing and reading, has taken a toll. More breaks during the day are required just to focus on something else for a while. Such is the life of a writer!

Despite the challenges that come with aging, I have maintained a resilient spirit and a determination to continue pursuing my passion for writing. Each obstacle I face serves as a reminder of the strength and perseverance that live within me. As I navigate the complexities of growing older, I find solace in the power of words and the catharsis they bring.

Embracing the changes that come with age, I am reminded of the wisdom and experience that accompany each passing year. Through my writing, I have encapsulated my journey, immortalizing moments of joy, sorrow, and everything in between. As I reflect on the chapters of my life, I am grateful for the opportunity to share my story with others and leave an enduring legacy through my words.

Amid physical limitations and the inevitable effects of time, I find comfort writing, a timeless form of expression that transcends the boundaries of age. With each word I pen, I defy the constraints of my years and embrace the boundless potential that lies within me. As I continue to navigate the complexities of aging, I am reminded that the true measure of a writer lies not in the years they have lived, but in the stories they have yet to tell.

God bless each of you on your journey today.

Also by Dr. Cravey

Whispers on the Wind

Eli and the Rod of God

Christian Perspectives on the Modern World

Skid Marks (a novel)

The Whispering Trees (a novel)

Living Parables: Grace in Every Chapter

At the Crossroads

Living Sermons

Heartstrings of Faith

A Spiritual Fork in the Road

The Deepest Treasure (Children's Book)

Bobby Butts and Mr. Crow (Children's Book)

The Road Less Traveled

Lessons Learned: In the School of Hard Knocks

Paradigms and Parables

www.ingramcontent.com/pod-product-compliance
Lightning Source LLC
LaVergne TN
LVHW091217080426
835509LV00009B/1033